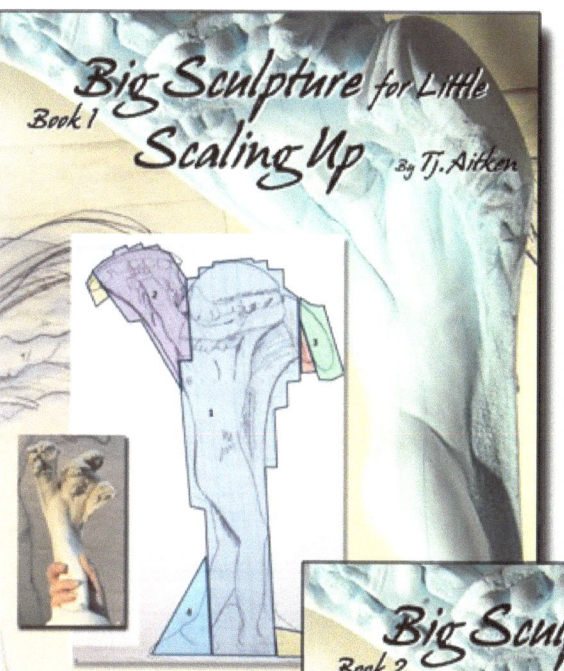

Big Sculpture for Little
Book 1
Scaling Up By T.J. Aitken

Big Sculpture for Little
Book 2
Carving Foam By T.J. Aitken

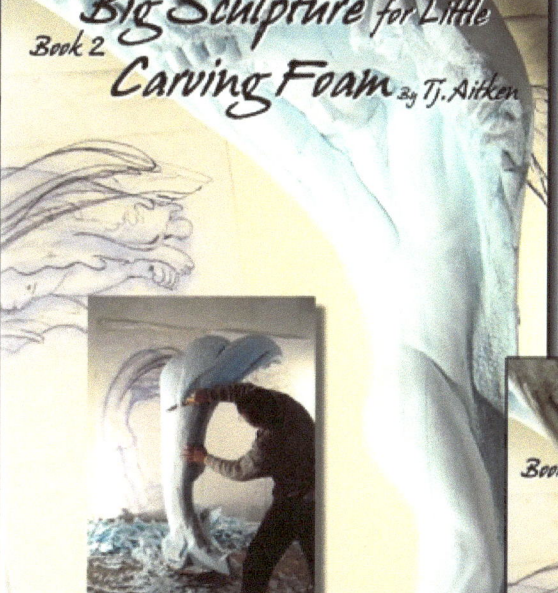

Big Sculpture for Little
Book 3
Stone Coating By T.J. Aitken

Get the entire set, available at:
www.SculptureByTj.com

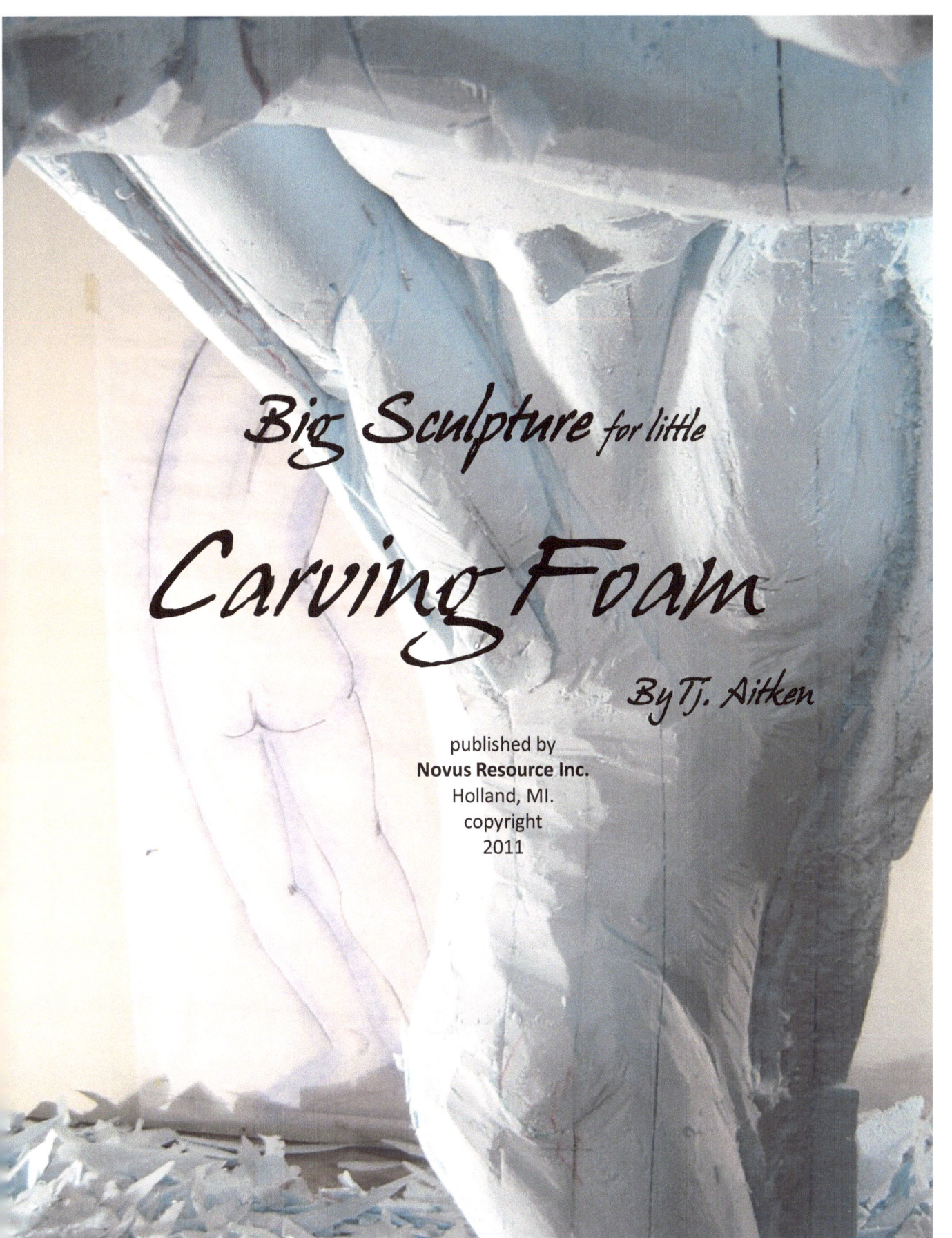

Big Sculpture *for little*

Carving Foam

By T.J. Aitken

published by
Novus Resource Inc.
Holland, MI.
copyright
2011

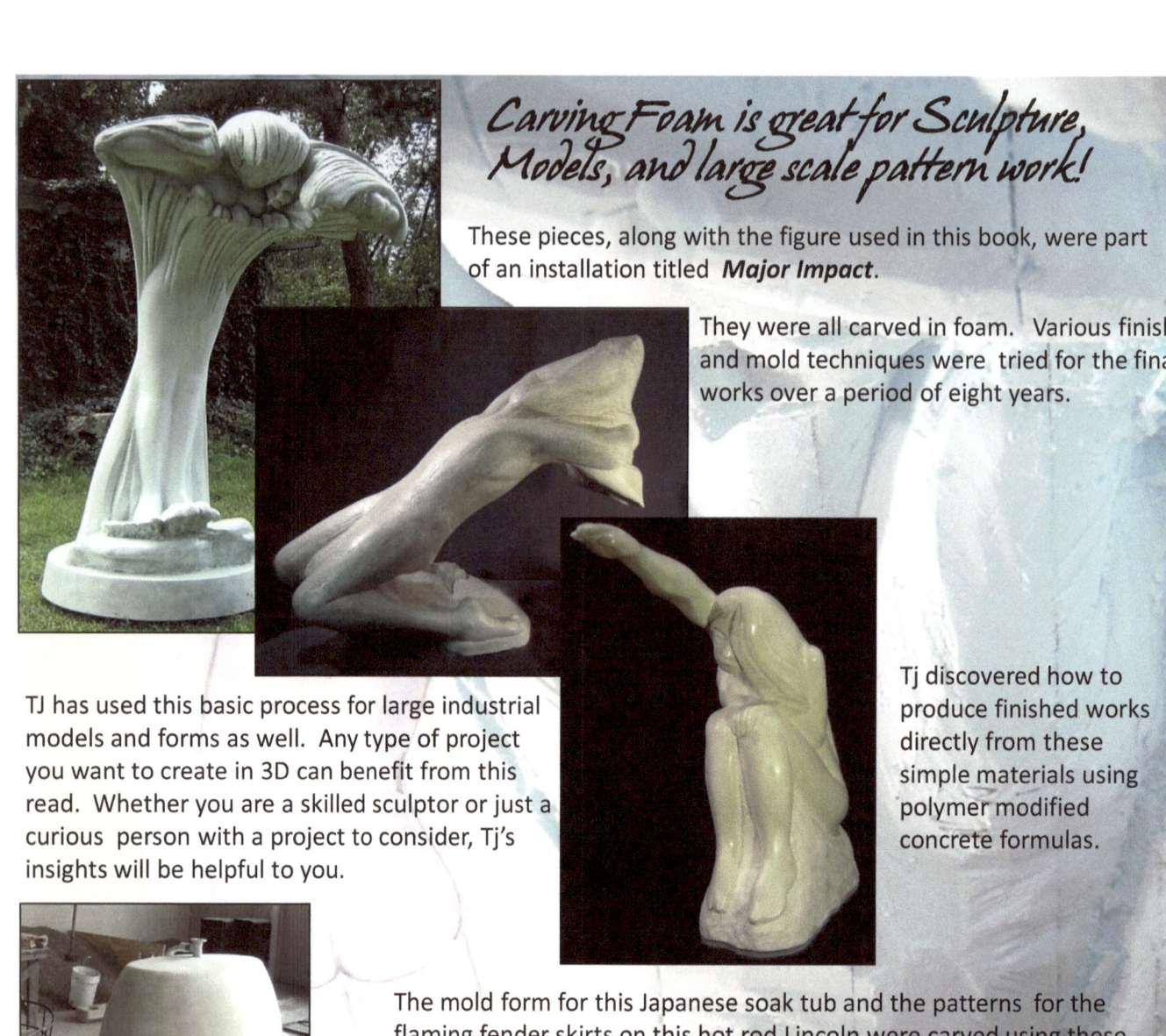

Carving Foam is great for Sculpture, Models, and large scale pattern work!

These pieces, along with the figure used in this book, were part of an installation titled **Major Impact**.

They were all carved in foam. Various finish and mold techniques were tried for the final works over a period of eight years.

TJ has used this basic process for large industrial models and forms as well. Any type of project you want to create in 3D can benefit from this read. Whether you are a skilled sculptor or just a curious person with a project to consider, Tj's insights will be helpful to you.

Tj discovered how to produce finished works directly from these simple materials using polymer modified concrete formulas.

The mold form for this Japanese soak tub and the patterns for the flaming fender skirts on this hot rod Lincoln were carved using these same techniques.

To the sculptor:

The 3 book series is a step by step explanation for creating big sculpture for very little money. Tj's studio photographs and notes have been laid out to best show the process he developed over several years. The text includes discussion on tools and techniques as they are used on the pieces, as well as errors and how to fix them. All three books are intended as studio guides for experienced sculptors, yet they stress simple, inexpensive tools and materials. Some items reappear from earlier books for the artist who has just that volume. The final book illustrates the formula developed for stone coating the pieces with a new process using polymer modified concrete.

Content - The Carving Process Outlined

Creating a Block for carving the piece (covered in Book 1, *Scaling Up*)

About foam		7
Tools and their uses		9
1.	Lay out, line work, basic carving technique	12
2.	Sneaking up on the form	14
	Fixtures for holding	17
3.	Hogging	19
	Viewing the work	20
4.	Carving major forms	21
	Adding on to the block	22
	Carving progression-	24
5.	Errors oversights and additions	25
6.	Piecing in intricate areas	29
	Finishing methods & materials choices-	39
7.	Sanding	40
8.	Gaps	42

Coating the Piece This process is in *Book 3, Stone Coating*

Book 2 *Carving Foam*

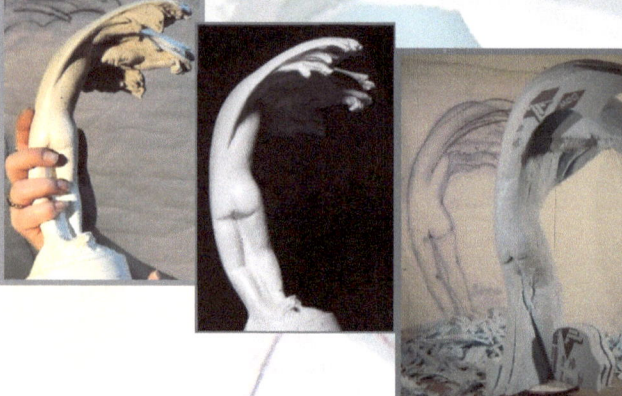

A low cost way to make large sculptural objects

In **Book *1, Scaling Up*** we began the walk through the process with maquette photos, control drawings and block construction.

This book continues with:

-Tools and techniques for carving and working with foam

-Tricks for templating, viewing and detailing the piece

-Alternatives for finishing

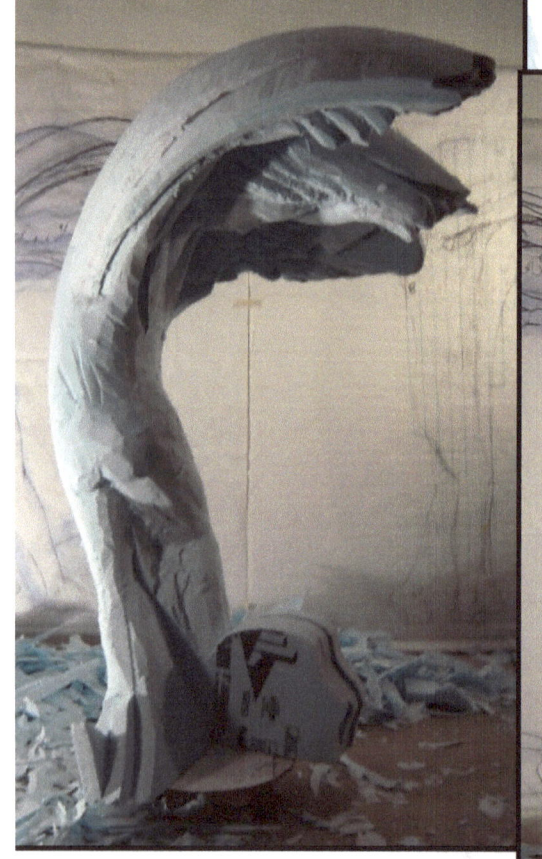

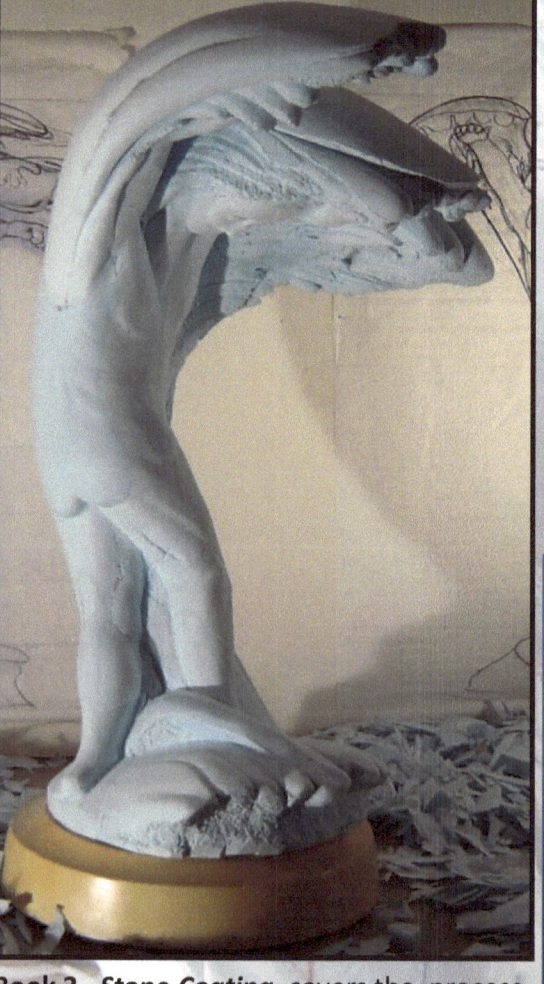

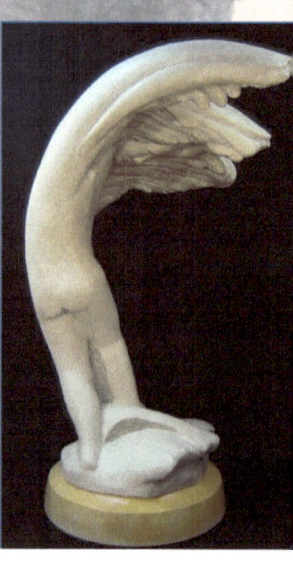

Book 3, *Stone Coating* covers the process of finishing with polymer modified cement.

Advantage of Foam

Foam is often thought of as a cheap, weak material. It is inexpensive and you can snap an appendage easily, but in compression this stuff is fantastic. It will hold hundreds of pounds of force. Cheap means that you can use a lot for larger pieces and afford to throw away scrap and mistakes. Speed is a huge plus. Foam can be cut, glued and shaped extremely quickly, enabling a sculpture to proceed at a rapid pace. The fidelity that you can get with a little practice is astonishing. Dow extruded foam plank will sand to a smooth surface that will satisfy most pattern making needs. It is available at your DIY store.

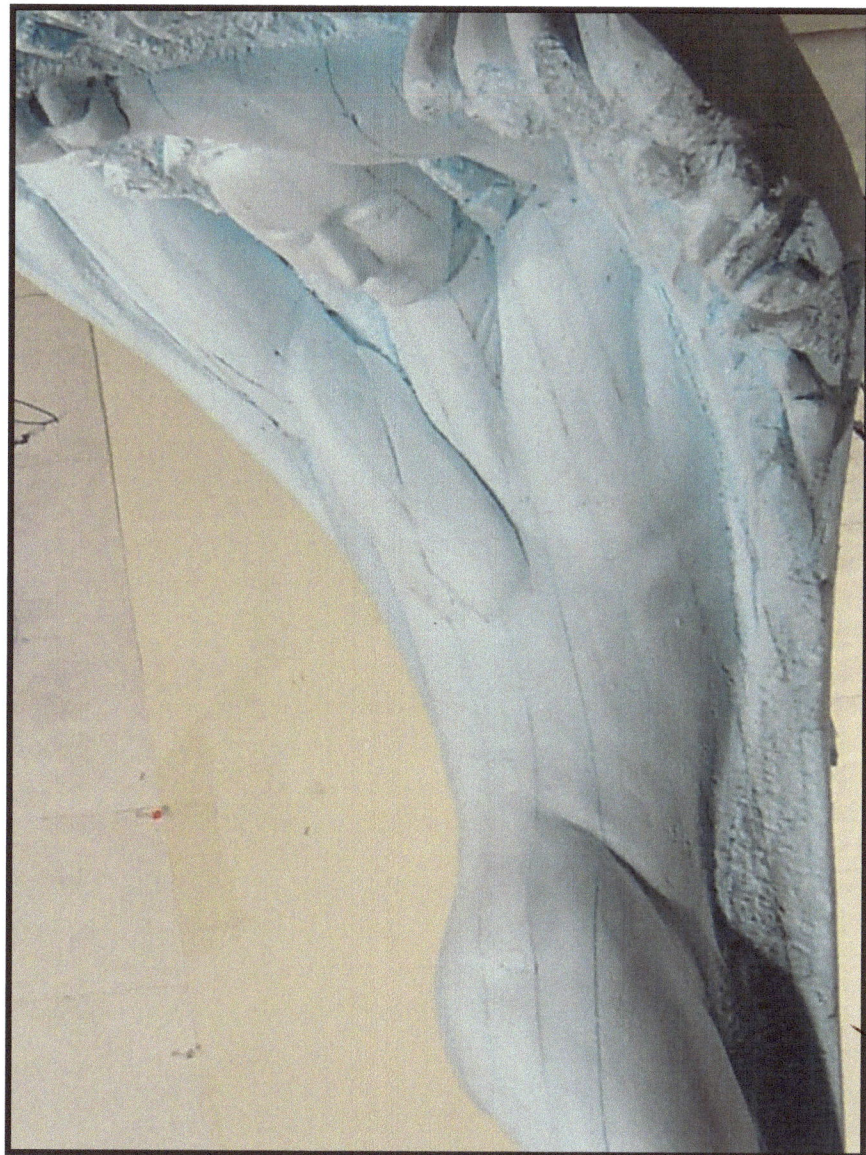

There are certain techniques required for working with foam. It must be handled with a delicate touch when carving and sanding to avoid "tearing". Once you have most of the surface complete you must be careful not to scar it before the surface coat goes on. But practice will make you good at this.

Changing your piece is also quite easy. Cut away, flatten the area and glue in a new piece. Your change is done in minutes. Light weight means easy lifting, moving and repositioning with no heavy equipment needed.

The final advantage comes from breakthroughs in concrete formulas. With a thin skin of glass-filled, polymer-modified cement, your foam carving becomes a light weight rock, able to withstand a lot more abuse than you would think due to great compressive strength.

About Foam - The Nature and Applications of these Materials

There are two common types: **Polyurethane**, and **Polystyrene**. Urethanes are impervious to solvents and can be used with any type of resins, paints and finishing materials (polyester boat resins and bondo for example). Styrene is way more sensitive to solvents and you can't go near it with acetone, lacquer thinner, polyester resin, or many other solvents. It will dissolve. (I have a funny story about this from Italy, but that's for another day). This is why you must be careful with glue. Incredibly, epoxy resins and alcohol (which dissolves unhardened epoxy and shellac) are fine to use with styrene. Urethane foam is generally yellow. You can buy urethane as a 2 part liquid which, when mixed together, foam up several times the volume of liquid and then sets and becomes rigid. It can be purchased in sheet and block but it is expensive. This document will not cover urethanes. There are also **open cell, closed cell** and **bead board** types of foam, which will not be covered completely here.

Styrene bead is the cheaper stuff that you recognize from coffee cups and those cheap coolers you see in pieces along the road and washing up at the beach. These items are fragile and easily trashed. Bead board is made by expanding styrene beads with steam in a closed chamber or mold where they stick together. Mass produced Items are done like this. Floatation and construction materials are produced in huge chambers. If there is a company like this near by, you might consider getting thick blocks to work with. But the quality can be difficult. Bead board with greater density can carve fairly well but it is hard to find. Most of the bead board at the hardware store is crumbly and only suitable for insulation.

Extruded styrene foam is much tougher, has virtually no voids and carves beautifully. This stuff has a small closed cell that is not crumbly and holds a shape very well. It can be sanded to a very nice surface quickly and is readily available at building material outlets. It is usually pink or blue, and not the common white of bead board. It comes in ½ to 2" thicknesses and can be purchased in some areas in thicker billet blocks for dock floatation.

Gluing Styrene Foam

Styrene can be stuck to itself and other materials with contact cements that do not have solvents that attack it. (***Always test*** *before trying anything new).* 3M Spray 77 is my choice. It will dissolve styrene if applied too thick, but if sprayed in a nice even thin coat to both surfaces and allowed to tack up it will stick them together very well. The bite makes the bond pretty permanent. You can use 5 minute epoxy as well but any hard material like this in a glue joint will make carving a nightmare. You cannot get a good surface across a glue joint unless the glue is about the same hardness as the foam. 3M spray 78 is made for foam and will not dissolve it. This and 3M spray 90 however have a bigger nozzle orifice and come out in greater quantity. You will use more glue and not get any better adhesion with either. I have tried a few other types but the 77 seems to work best and most consistently.

Perfect fit, even thorough spray coverage and tack time are important to a solid joint. Fit your pieces carefully. (I put little tick marks across the joint to aid in alignment). Clean off all crumbs, you don't want anything but glue in the joint. Spray both pieces, let the glue tack up. (When it is not liquid, but still sticky). Then align and squeeze them together and pound the materials to squash out the air and distribute the glue. Sometimes clamping is helpful. Once a broad amount of surface has contacted there is little chance for adjustment, so placement is tricky, but a little practice and some markings will make it easy. The set is instant and you can go immediately to the next piece. You will not be able to pull most joints apart without tearing foam. You will get small gaps. (Not to worry. There are techniques for dealing with this).

Carving Foam- The Knife

Foam is so easy to carve that it will amaze you. If you know where you are going you can get a form quickly. I recommend a maquette study so you are very sure where you are going. Foam is delicate, so finesse is very important. But the piece will be surprisingly tough when you are all done. Only small appendages are subject to breakage and your only real enemy is a blow that will dent or scar the surface.

 The key to carving is the sharp blade. I use this "Old Hickory" eight inch butcher knife. It will need sharpening about every hour of work. A very sharp blade which is drawn through the material in a slicing motion will cleanly take out a ½ inch thick slice about a foot long. As long as the blade is in a slicing motion it will not tear the foam. If the sideways slicing action stops, and you just push it, the foam will get a raggedy edge. With a little practice you can take off a 1 ½ inch corner 20 inches long in one stroke, or feather slice a millimeter from a surface to fair in a contour. A slight twist sideways will break off a piece for fast work.

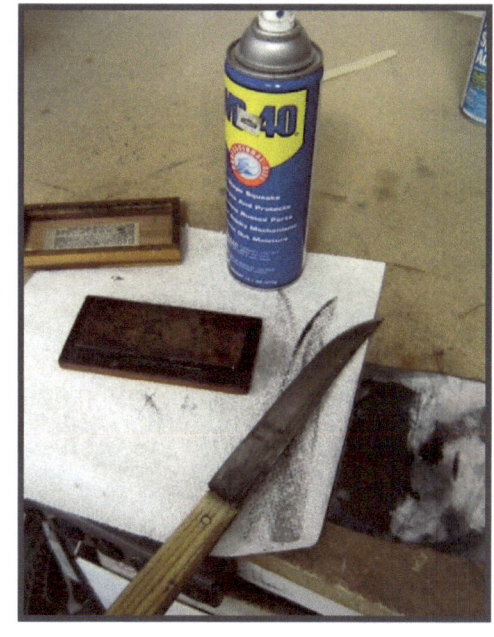

Sharp, Sharpen, Sharper!

Some WD 40 on a Washita stone will let you hone the blade to scalpel capability. Some 220 grit wet-dry sand paper and turpentine will clean the sides and remove glue.

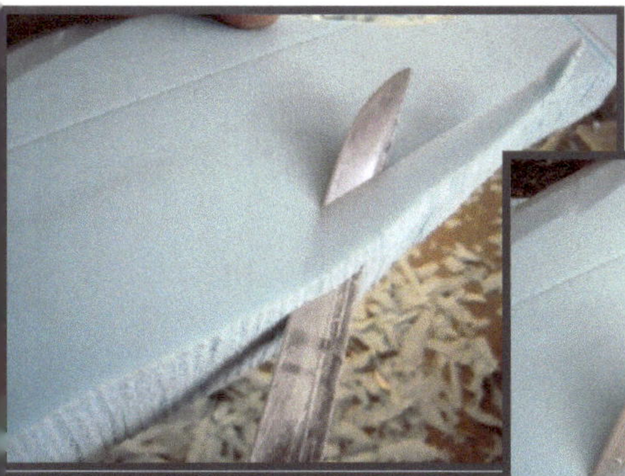

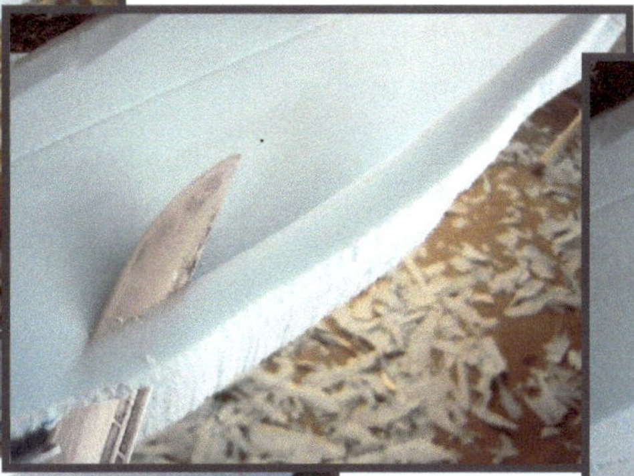

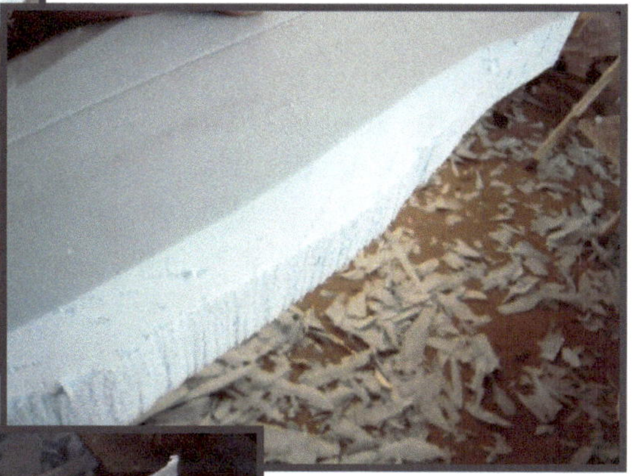

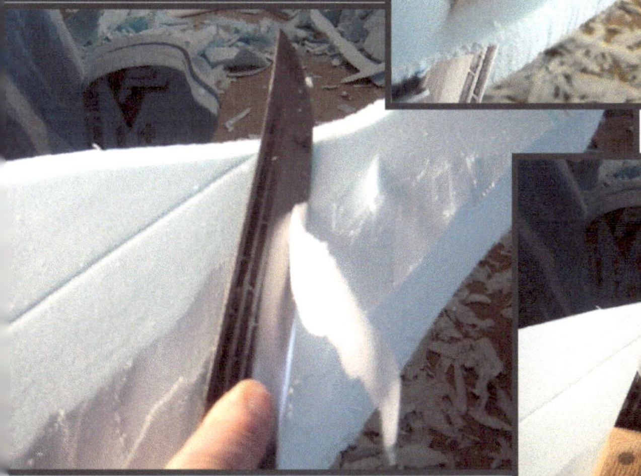

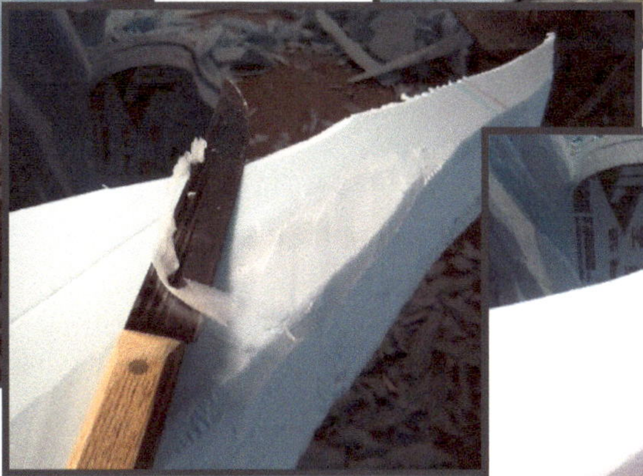

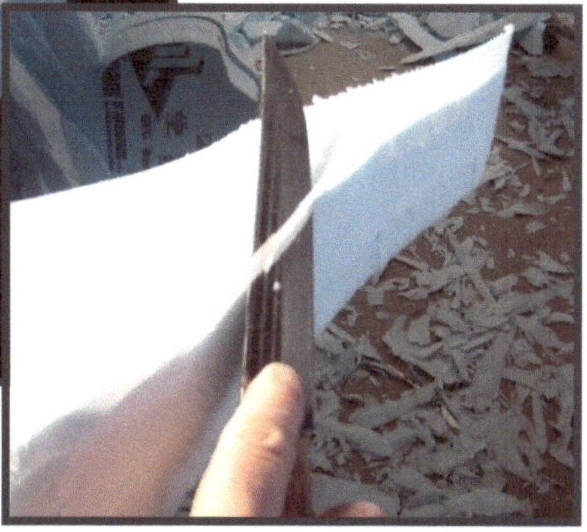

With your forefinger on top you can
 push and slice to achieve very accurate
control, and very thin slices.

Tools for Carving Foam

Here are some of the other things to use:

1. The **Exacto knife** is the primary detail tool. I am constantly cutting to my lines with it and typically making a V cut for crisp detail.

2. The **interchangeable handle tool** is handy with hooked blade options but only occasionally will you use one of the other blades. These will all cut without crumbs.

3. The **depth cutter** is a home made block with a blade inserted. If you need precise depth we can adjust the blade position. A radius edge allows a rocking motion for slicing. Some tight places need other sorts of thin blades.

4. Some **serrated kitchen utensils** to call on rarely.

5. A **melon carver** is good for gouging out negative space but makes crumbs and leaves a crumbly surface.

6. **Saws** will cut new planks and occasionally cut off larger areas of stock. A keyhole saw is very good for this. The black handle one has an adjustable swivel handle which helps in tight places.

7. A **surf form** is used only rarely. This will tear the surface and you will have to use other tools to tune it after carving. Only when it is hard to reach with a knife is this of value.

8. Finally the serrated **plaster hook** is one I use to intentionally tear a surface for a textured effect or occasionally to gouge out a deep pocket.

Tools for Sanding Foam

Always carve as much as possible instead of abrading. You move faster, eat less dust and get more skilled with the blades at detailed work. When you just can't go finer by carving then use abrasives. The old **auto body sanding board** and 36 grit paper can be very handy on a large area requiring a smooth surface. It does tear slightly but it unifies surface and the results can be hidden by stone coating or fine finished with finer grit.

The **spindle sander tubes** in different diameters are very helpful in detail areas along with **blocks and boards** of various shapes to help get into areas and refine surfaces. Little **wedges** with paper glued with 3M 77 can do wonders. I have even glued sand paper to some curved **modeling tools** to get into intricate details.

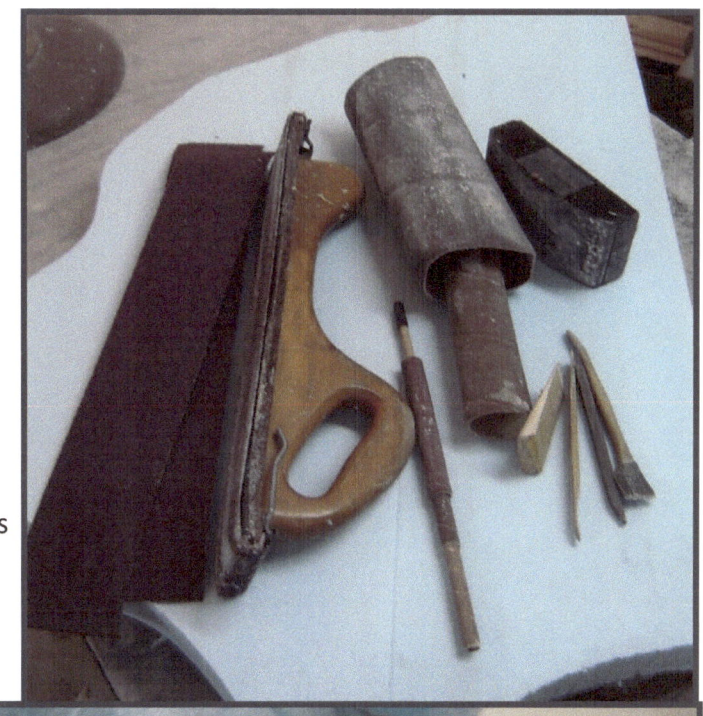

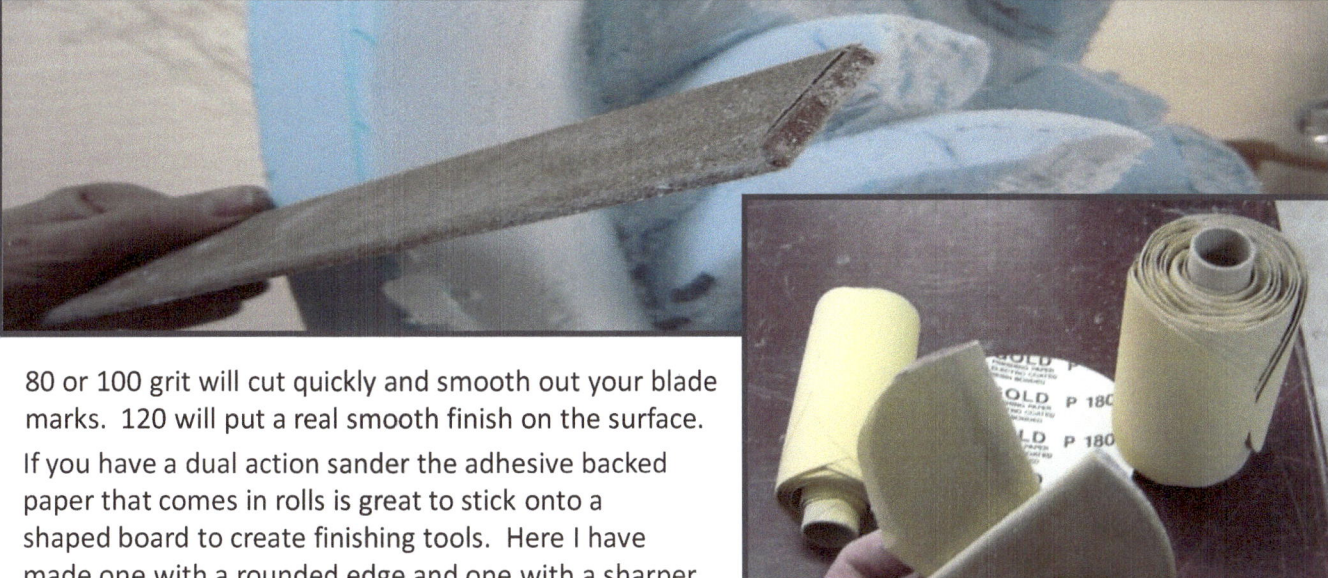

80 or 100 grit will cut quickly and smooth out your blade marks. 120 will put a real smooth finish on the surface.

If you have a dual action sander the adhesive backed paper that comes in rolls is great to stick onto a shaped board to create finishing tools. Here I have made one with a rounded edge and one with a sharper pointed edge for getting into details.

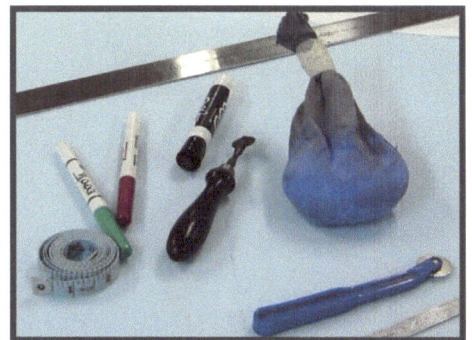

Marking Tools:
Before carving always mark the surface to know where to carve.
Dry erase markers will not dissolve the foam like a sharpie or permanent marker.
A **Pounce wheel** is commonly used to perforate paper sewing patterns. This is great for transferring a line from drawing to foam either with clear plastic film or paper and chalk filled **pounce bag** (old sock).

Layout Technique -   Drawing Transfer

Here is a simple way to start a relief piece. The transfer technique is the same one used in the first book for the two view layout, but in a relief there is only one view. A composition was drawn on plastic film to the desired scale. The film is then pinned over the foam sheet and the lines transferred with the pounce wheel. Pounced dots are drawn over with dry erase marker. In this instance we cut the higher portion out completely to be mounted to another full plank.

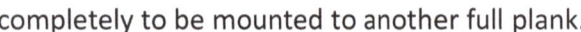

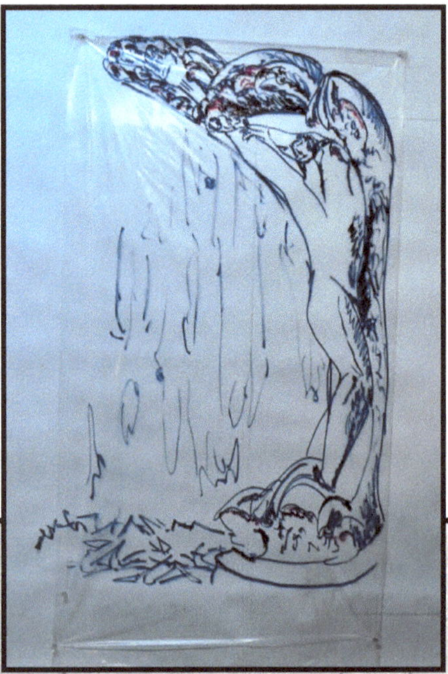

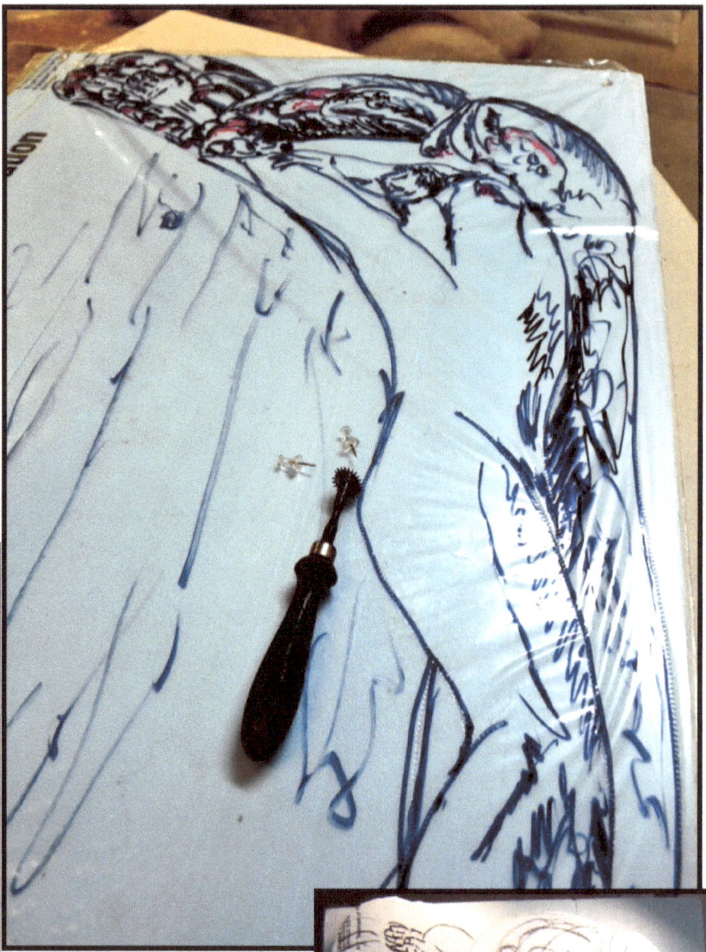

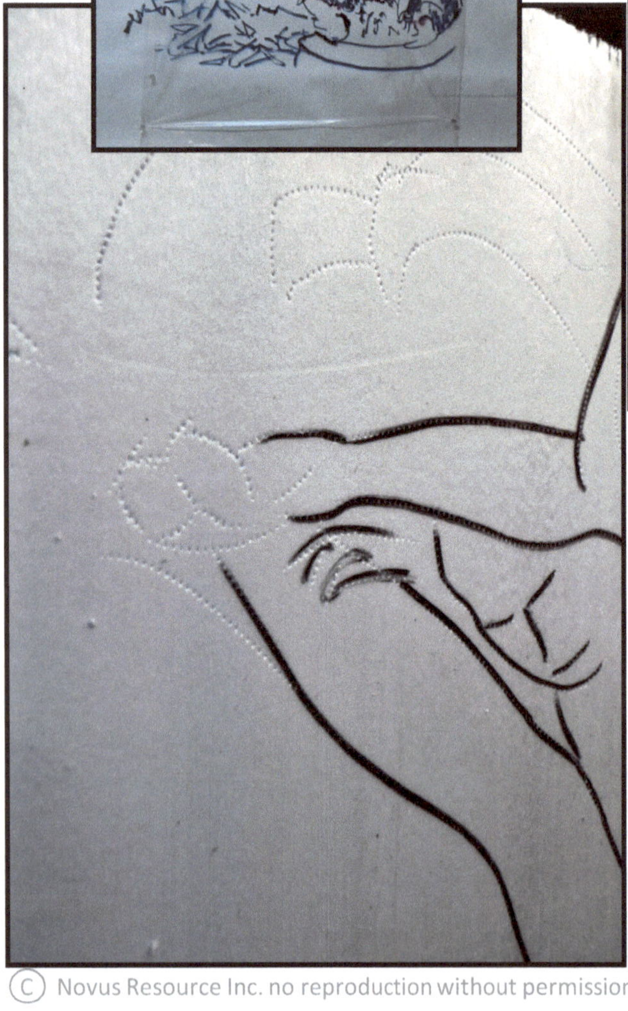

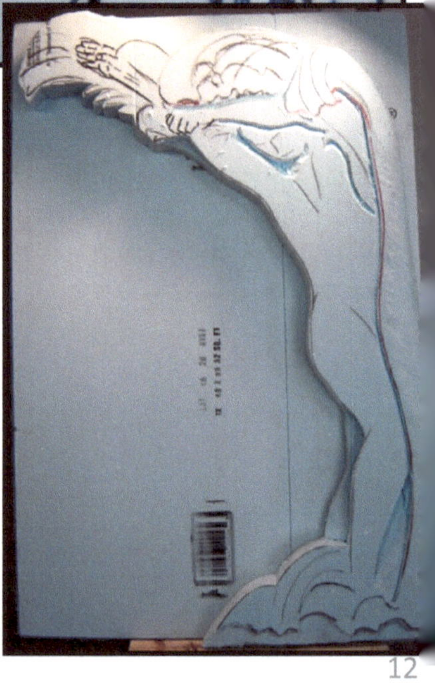

The composition can be constructed in layers that facilitate the process for carving and texture creation. The same film, once perforated, can be placed on another sheet and "pounced" with the chalk bag to create the same lines.

Carving Technique - Develop a Surface

Draw on the surface with the dry erase markers, and then cut to your lines. You want to refine your lines, then carve to them carefully.   If you define the highest areas in one color and use a second color for the rest you will have good indicators. On this relief piece the red lines are at the highest points. Some are ridges to be carefully cut and some are topographic high points that need avoidance while carving.   Cut the ridges first and determine how far down to go with adjacent areas.
All the forms are drawn on all the time until they are clearly visible from the carving.

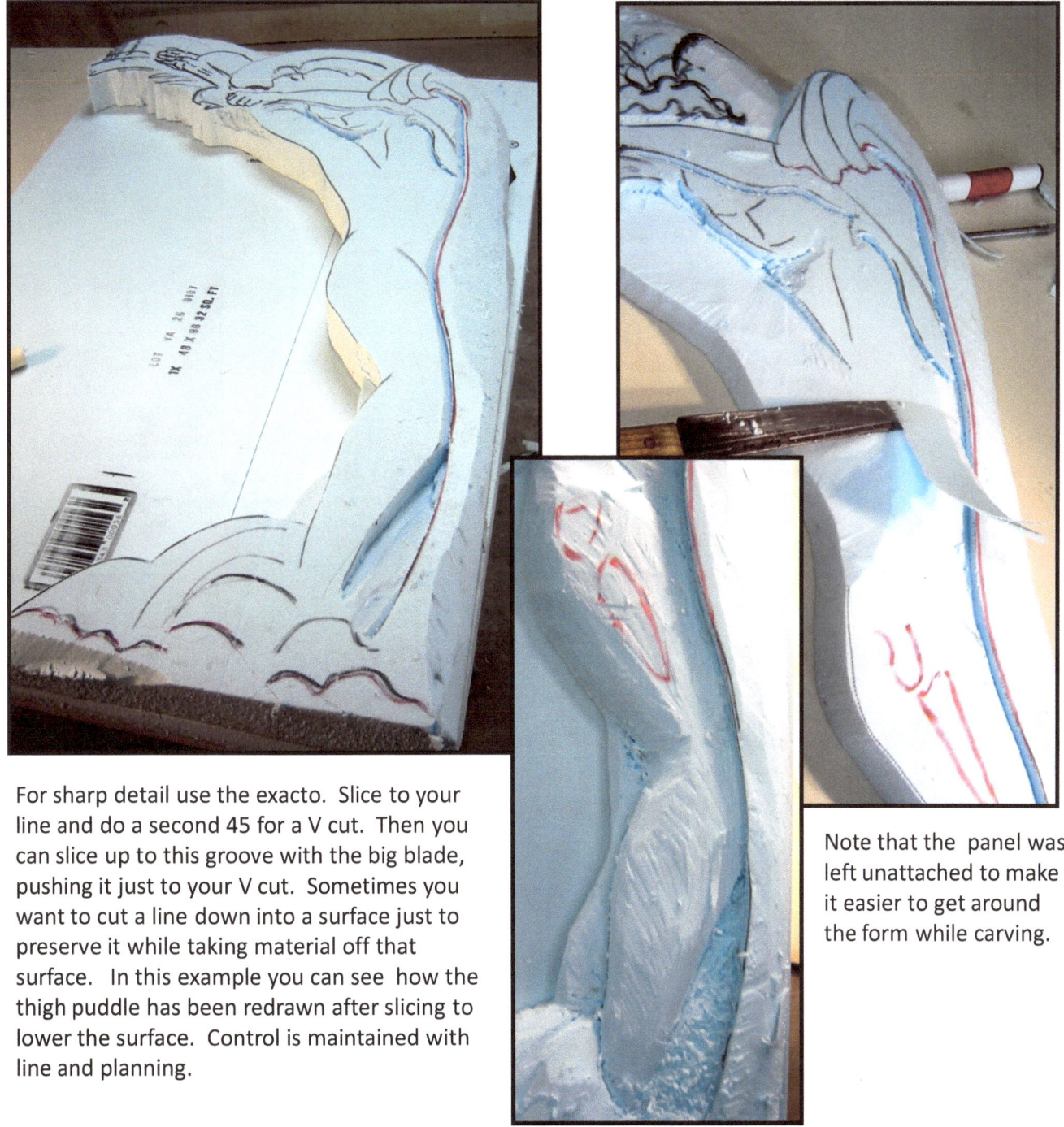

For sharp detail use the exacto. Slice to your line and do a second 45 for a V cut. Then you can slice up to this groove with the big blade, pushing it just to your V cut. Sometimes you want to cut a line down into a surface just to preserve it while taking material off that surface.   In this example you can see how the thigh puddle has been redrawn after slicing to lower the surface. Control is maintained with line and planning.

Note that the panel was left unattached to make it easier to get around the form while carving.

Surface Development in Steps - (Sneaking Up on it)

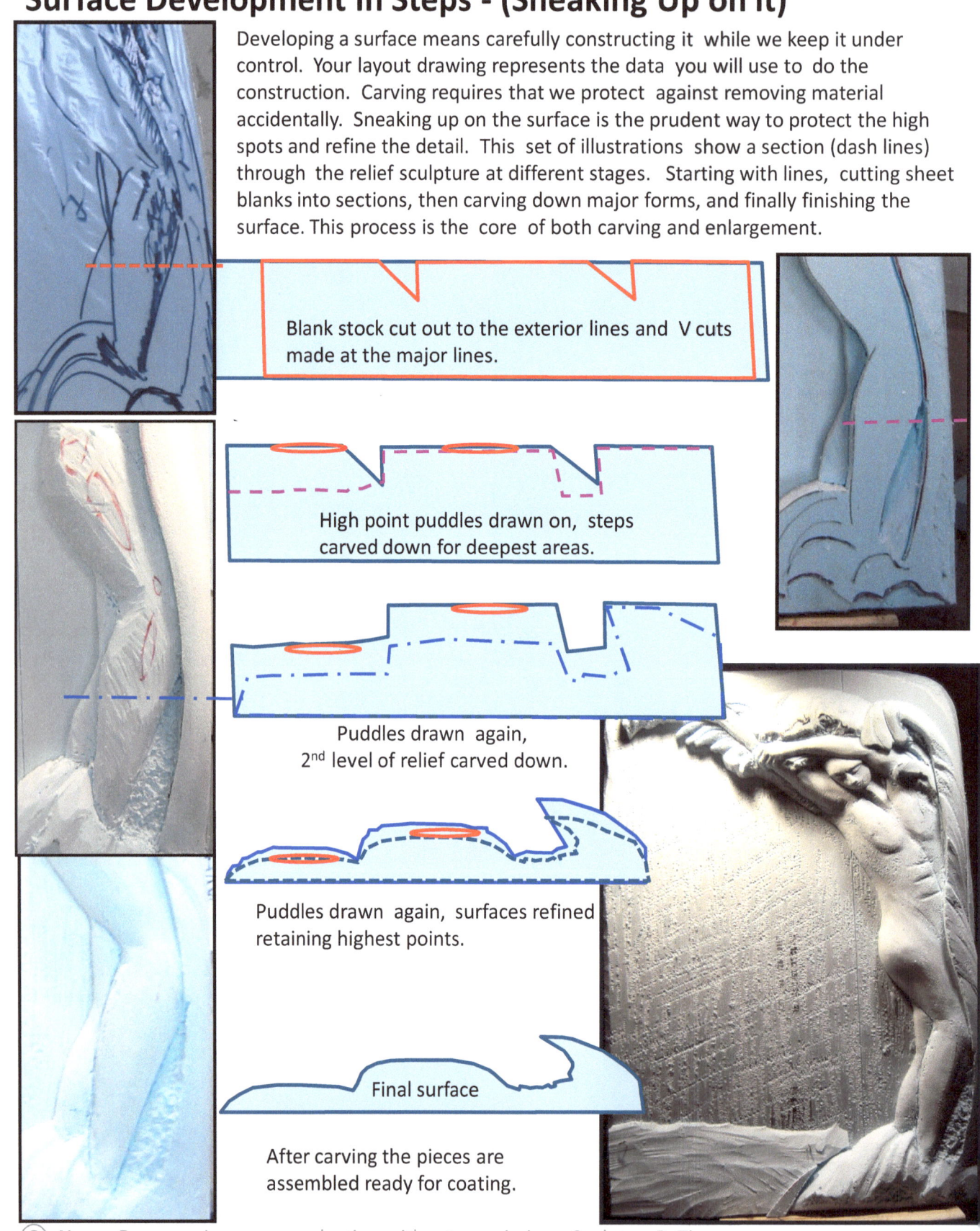

Developing a surface means carefully constructing it while we keep it under control. Your layout drawing represents the data you will use to do the construction. Carving requires that we protect against removing material accidentally. Sneaking up on the surface is the prudent way to protect the high spots and refine the detail. This set of illustrations show a section (dash lines) through the relief sculpture at different stages. Starting with lines, cutting sheet blanks into sections, then carving down major forms, and finally finishing the surface. This process is the core of both carving and enlargement.

Blank stock cut out to the exterior lines and V cuts made at the major lines.

High point puddles drawn on, steps carved down for deepest areas.

Puddles drawn again, 2nd level of relief carved down.

Puddles drawn again, surfaces refined retaining highest points.

Final surface

After carving the pieces are assembled ready for coating.

Are We Ready to Carve Foam?

You will need to have a block to start your piece. This process is covered in:

Book 1 *Scaling Up*
available at:
   SculptureByTj.com

Book 1 explains enlargement from a maquette using accurate layout techniques to make a control drawing in two views. Blocking strategies for gluing up planks into volumes are covered as well. Smaller works and relief pieces can be done more easily. Some of these examples are used here to illustrate carving techniques.

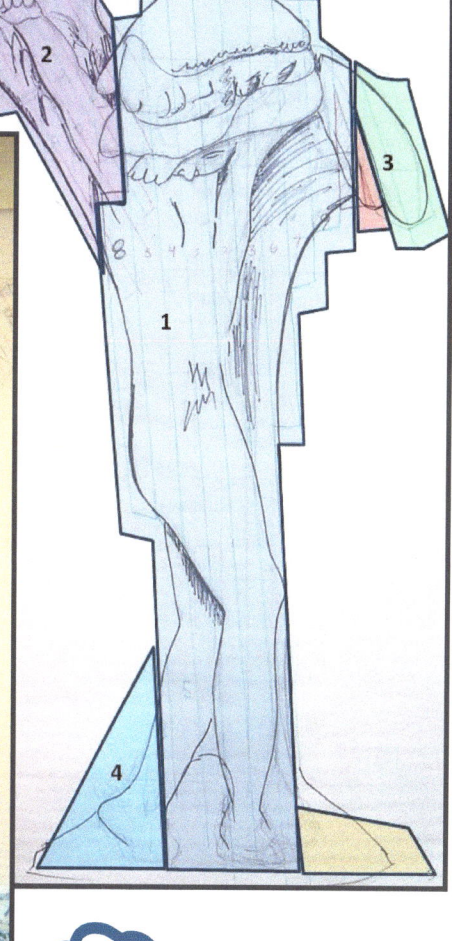

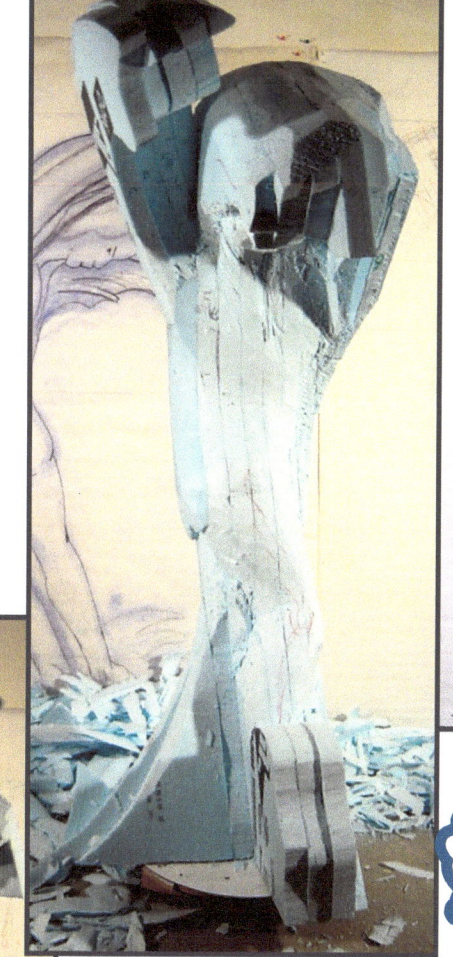

The basic process for creating a block is to laminate sections of extruded foam board together with 3M spray 77. Foam can be very strong in a block but the surface will dent with extreme clamping or pounding. Planning how you build can make the work go much faster. You will want to think through carving your piece and build the block to facilitate the work. Here some sections are intentionally left un-attached. Some areas at the base are left long and open to enable clamping and stabilizing. The red, green and yellow on the drawing above have not been added yet. This makes a flat surface for laying the piece on a bench for hogging.

Design for Carving

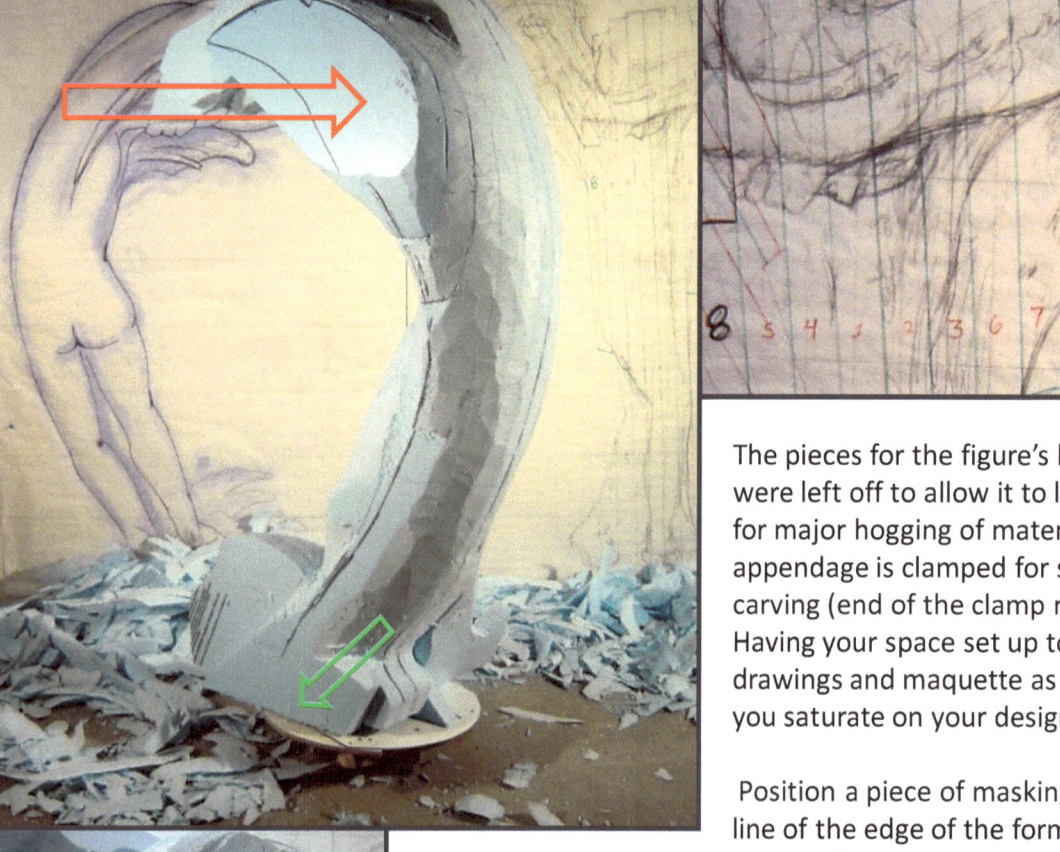

The pieces for the figure's left side appendage were left off to allow it to lay flat on the bench for major hogging of material. One appendage is clamped for support while carving (end of the clamp rests on the table). Having your space set up to view your drawings and maquette as you work will help you saturate on your design.

 Position a piece of masking tape to define the line of the edge of the form. Tape allows you to stand back and view the line from many angles and move sections of the line until you like it. You can also draw on the tape. Skinny black tape is really good for this but expensive.

Fixtures and Holding the Work for Carving

To start Hogging off major pieces the light foam will need to be stabile. A clamp occasionally helps. Early on don't be too worried about denting the surface but clamp pads (of foam) protect surface. Figuring out how to hold the work, and get at all the different places can be a challenge. After chasing it around the table we finally got a trash bag full of chips to set it in, like a bean bag chair.

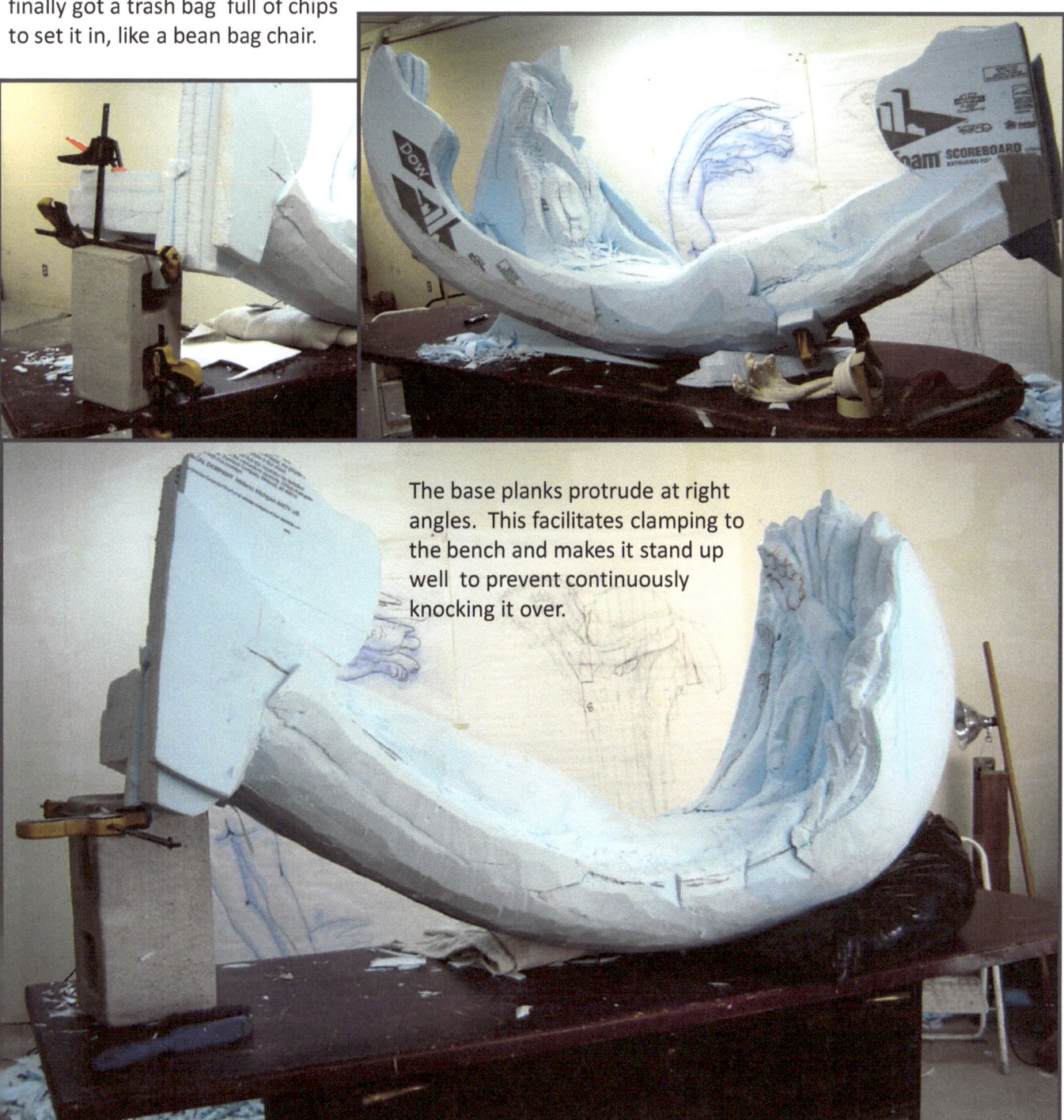

The base planks protrude at right angles. This facilitates clamping to the bench and makes it stand up well to prevent continuously knocking it over.

All the detail work was much easier to do in this position

*By the way, that is not a cement block, it is a piece of carved foam with a plastic coating. (Great fun to toss at someone)

The Craftsman's Internal Bell

Any time you are going to make a major move that is hard to turn back from, you should get a brain jolt. You are about to jump over a precipice and the bell goes off.

> -Did I check everything?
> -Am I sure of my direction?
> -Is there anything else I should deal with before I go?

When we're about to change processes, make a mold, paint a part, cut into a big piece of stock, or do any operation that **_can't easily be undone_**, pause and review the work plan to make sure we have left nothing out. Think down the road and consider what mistakes could be avoided. This has helped me countless times as I recall disasters and set backs from former projects.

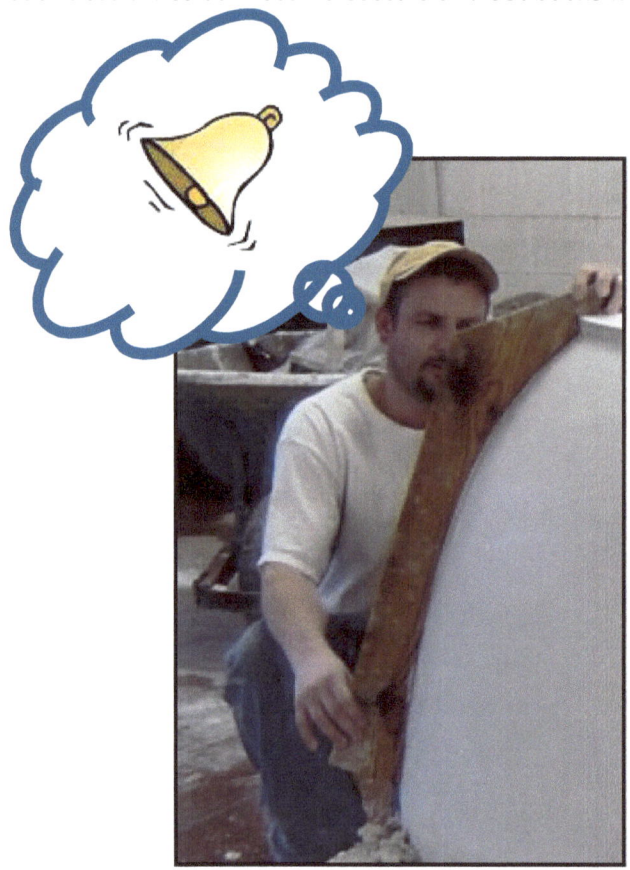

Even simple efficiencies save you time, like considering all that can be done with the piece in the current position. Are there any more operations that can be done in this position before I move it again? This simple thought process can save countless hours of rework and set up time. When you see the bell icon in this book it is a good place to review your moves and options! Like: Is my blocking strategy going to help my carving?

Hogging off Material   (getting the proportions and mass to read well)

Really thick sections are sawn off with the hole saw but most reduction is done with the carving knife. The great thing is, there is no dust! Only chips to collect up. Here the piece is lying on the flat side and I've started to hog off the corners. You slice and view, slice and view, practicing clean slices. Work down to your lines and go around the whole form sneaking up on the surface, taking away what seems most obvious.

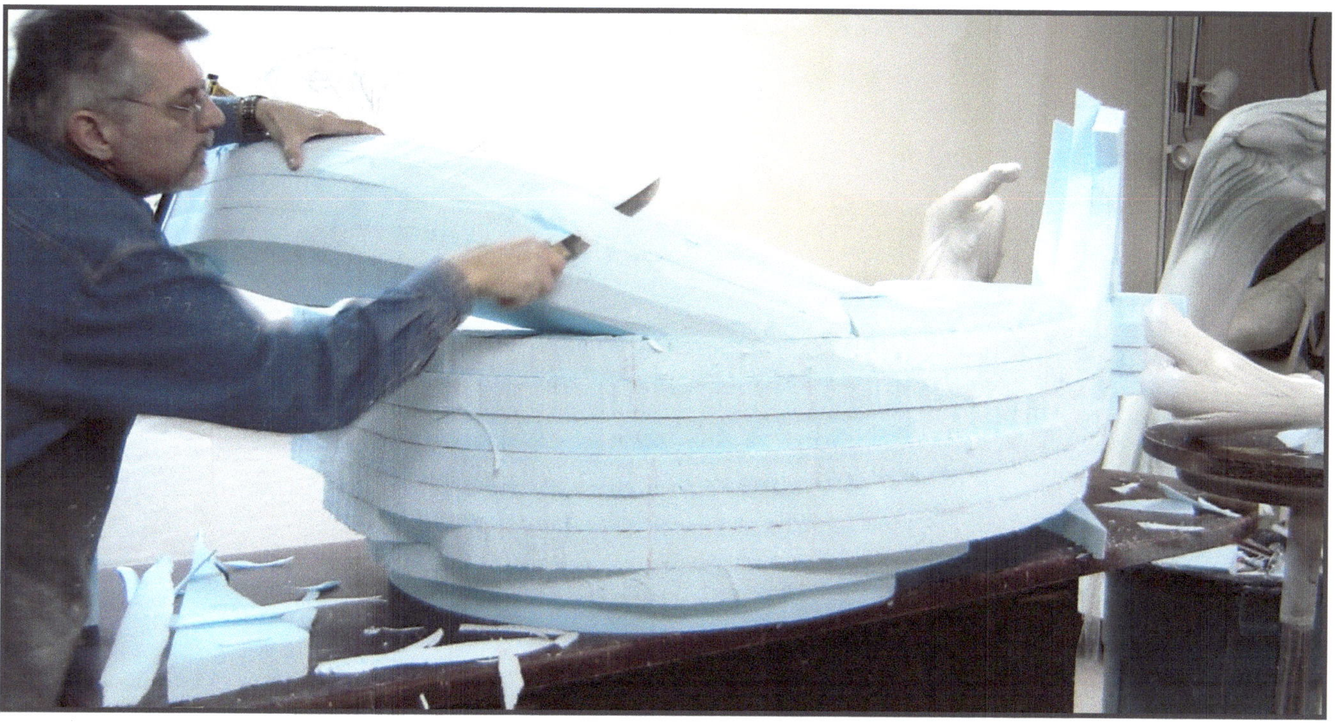

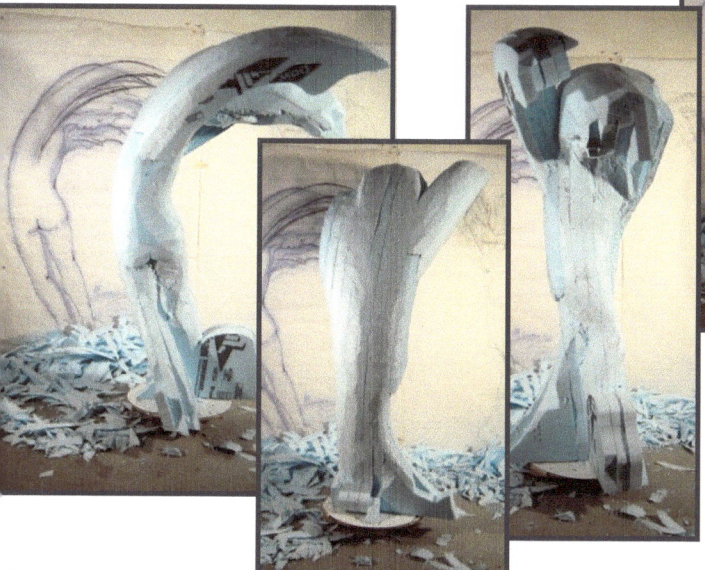

While carving, glue joints are not even noticeable with spray 77. You can glide over these with impunity. Early on, the fresh glue will build up on the blade causing sticking, but a quick wipe with solvent or 220 grit wet dry sandpaper will clean it back to slick again.
 In the early phase watch for glue joints that may need to be pressed again to close them up.

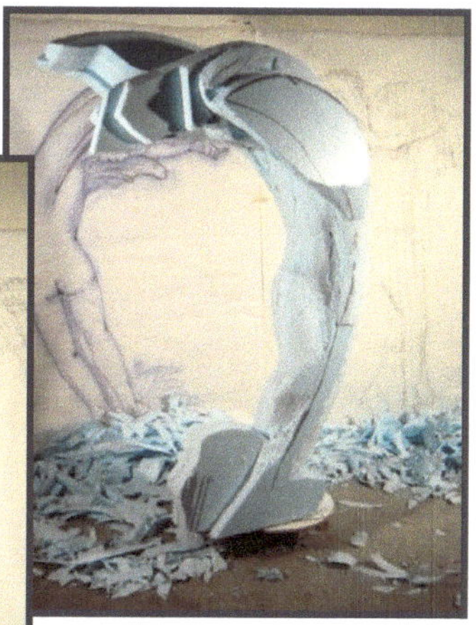

With 3D sculpture it is very important to view the work from all angles and compare lines, mass, shapes, and proportions. One tool that really helps me do this is an old electric department store display fixture that rotates slowly. This turntable is perfect for viewing a foam sculpture. I can sit in a comfy chair with the maquette at the same attitude as the work piece and rotate both of them comparing and stopping as new things come to mind. So many sculptures have only one good view and most have a bad side.

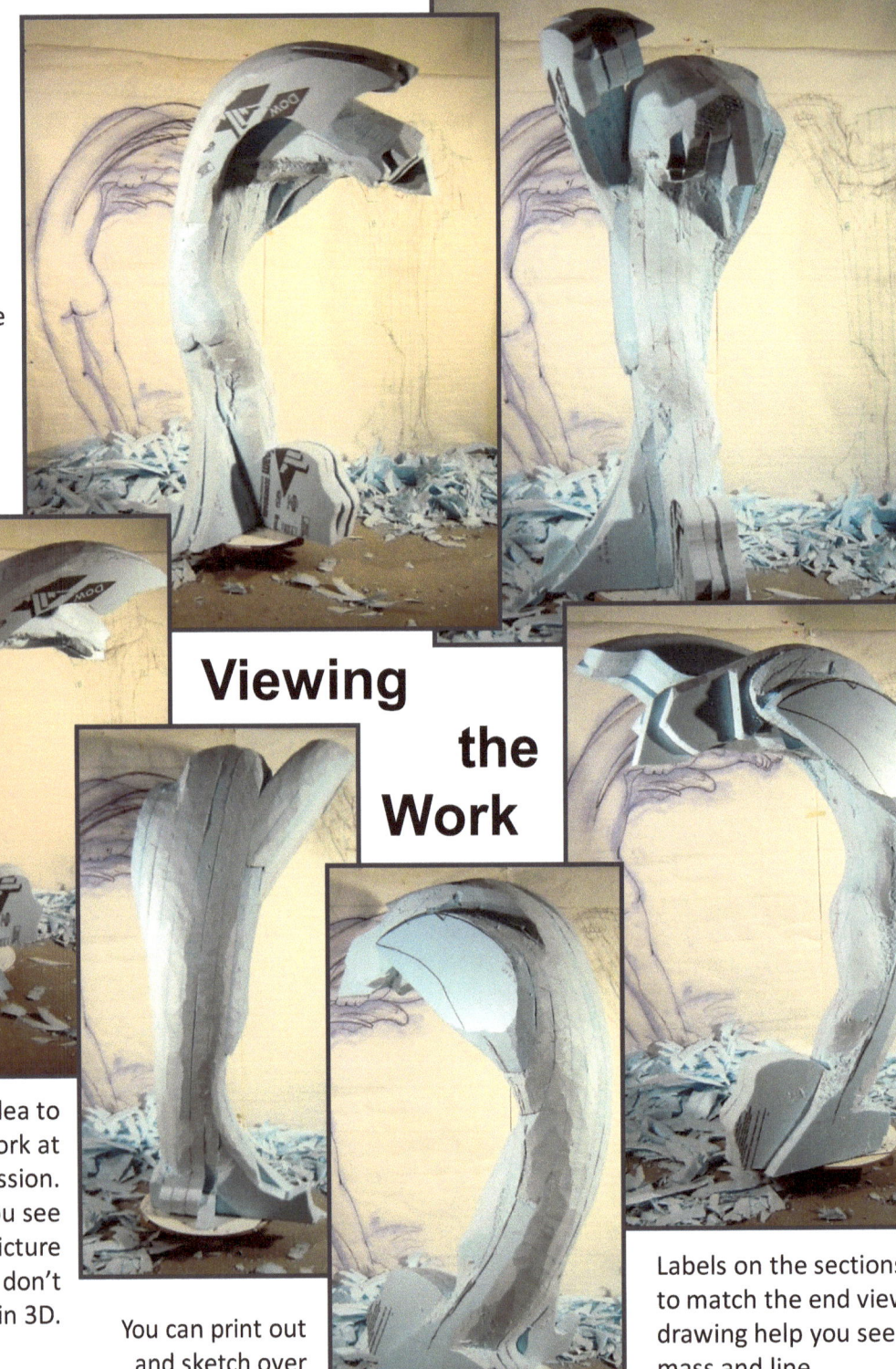

Strive to get all views to be at least interesting and always shoot for elegant composition.
A turntable will help you see. Use it often. Placing the work to view it against control drawings speeds decision making.

Viewing the Work

It is a good Idea to photo the work at the end of a session. Sometimes you see things in the picture that you don't notice in 3D.

You can print out and sketch over shots to devise solutions.

Labels on the sections to match the end view drawing help you see mass and line placement .

Carving Major Lines Against Secondary Forms

At this point you are blocking in major forms and getting your proportions and major lines where they need to be. Slice away material constantly checking the drawing, your work lines, and the maquette for reference. Try to keep section labels visible as long as possible and constantly place marks on the surface for guides. (The blue line along torso and leg represents edge of profile and needs to be cut in).

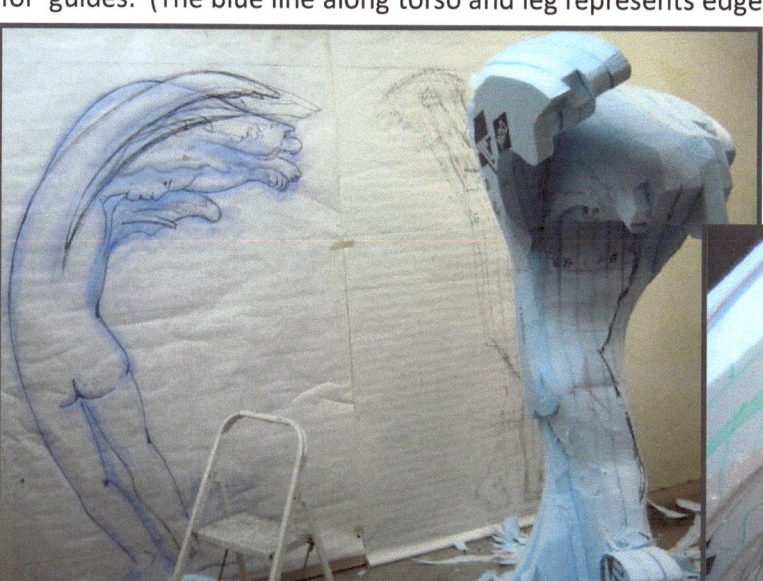

Bring the whole piece along at the same rate of refinement. It is important not to go too far in one area. This way, if you have to make a major change you do not loose too much effort.

Some lines come from a panel edge. Some are drawn on a surface and V cut, deepened and cut again after new detail is drawn on. (Note the start of wavy detail just below the red mark).

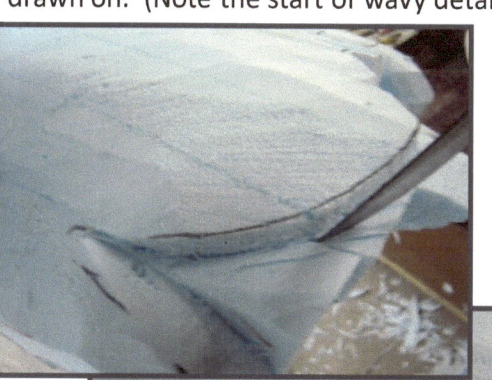

Here a major step has been defined and deepening the detail below has been started..

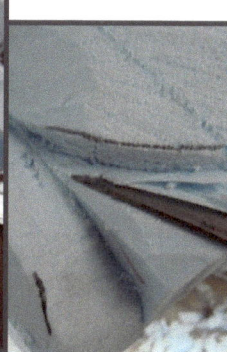

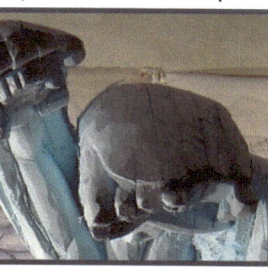

(Same area later).

Adding On-
Last Appendage

Hogging and major lines are complete. The work has been moved and fixtured, so we know how to handle it gently. Now that last appendage can be added. The plastic templating process is used for this addition after a look at the maquette. A line is drawn on the plastic which has been pinned on the piece. This allows you to see through the proposed piece to forms beyond and view the line from the other side. Do the pounce wheel perforation on the board stock and retrace the line for cutting like before.

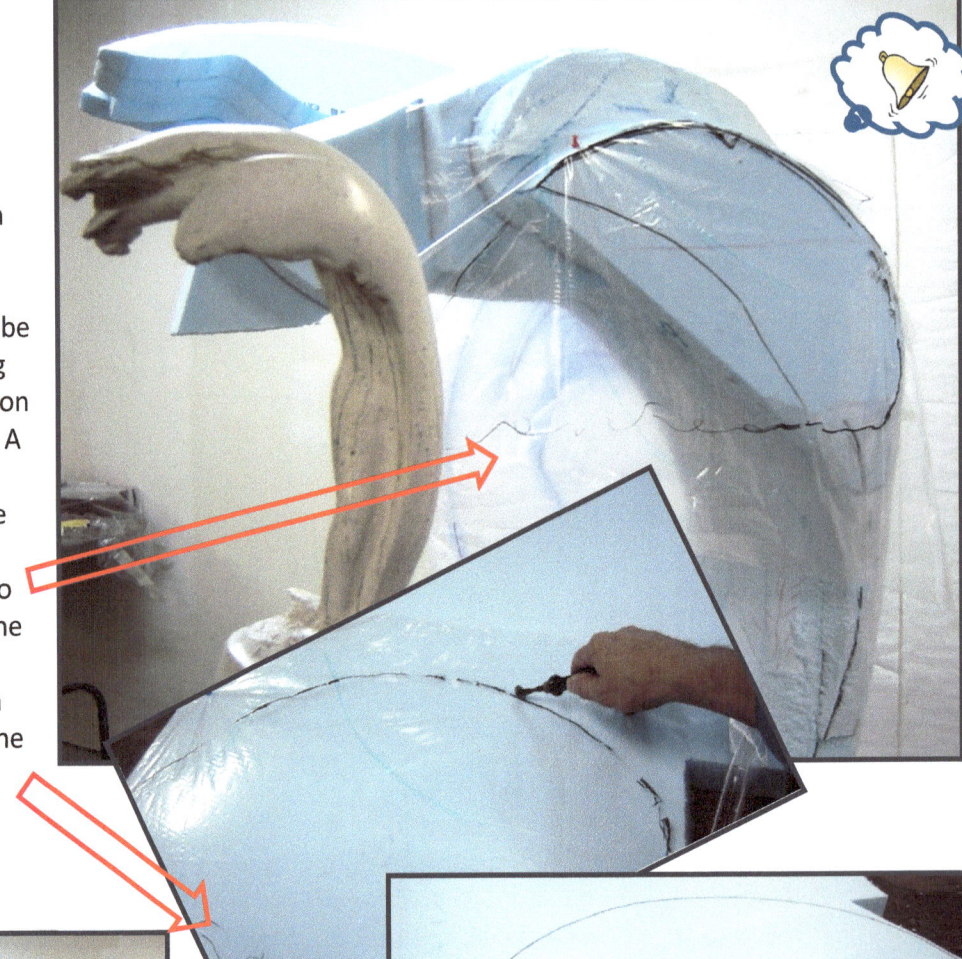

A healthy amount of stock is added for the lower edge, then the planks sections are cut.

The second piece was just made a little longer to give even more carving stock and all was glued up with 3M 77.

Carving

Most of the material is now laminated up and the more delicate carving begins. Draw anatomical guidelines on the surface and whittle away with the carving knife. Constantly view it from all angels and place the piece on the bench as needed to facilitate the work.

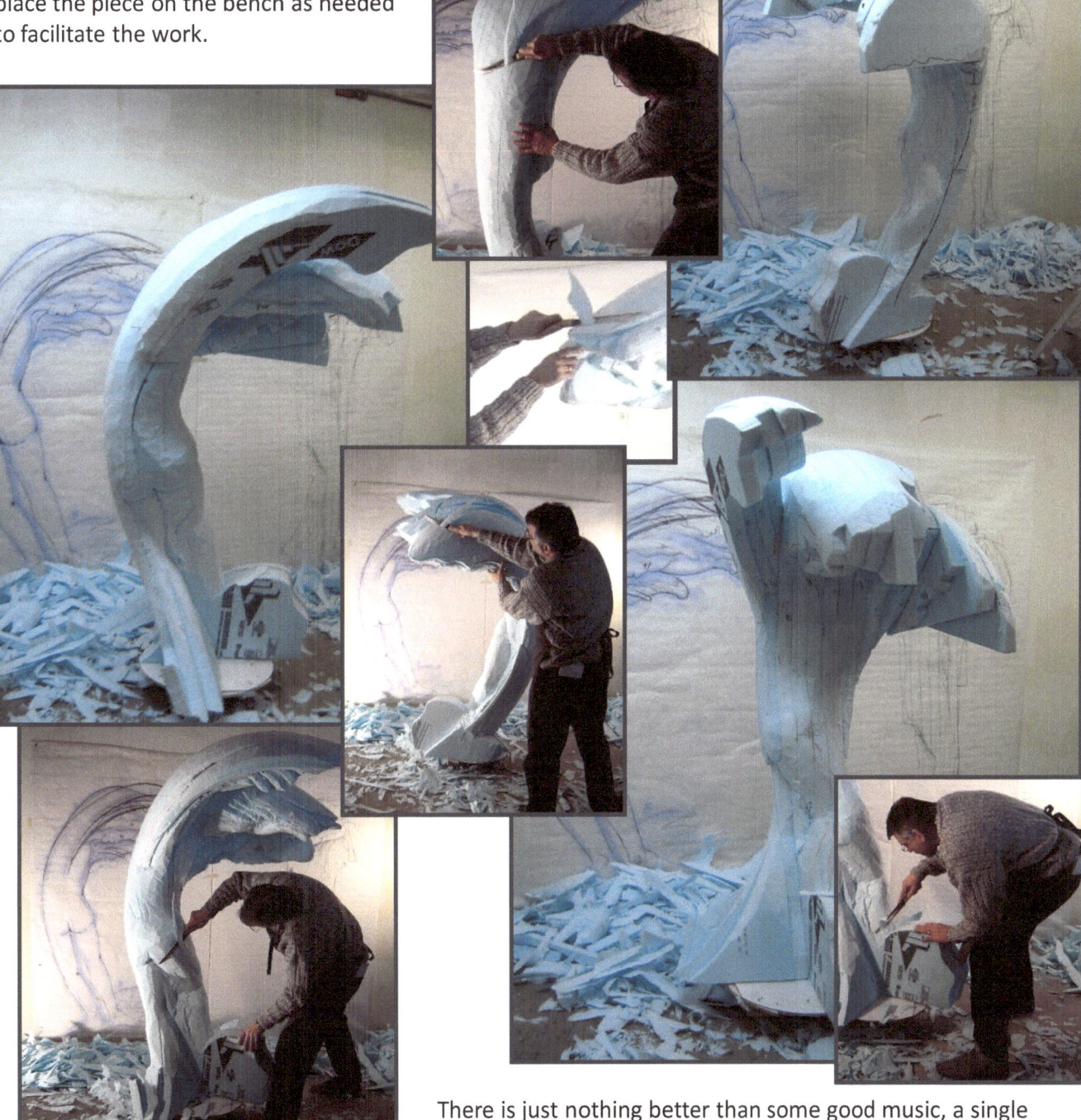

There is just nothing better than some good music, a single light source, and a carving session of groovin ' and smoothin', usually late into the night.

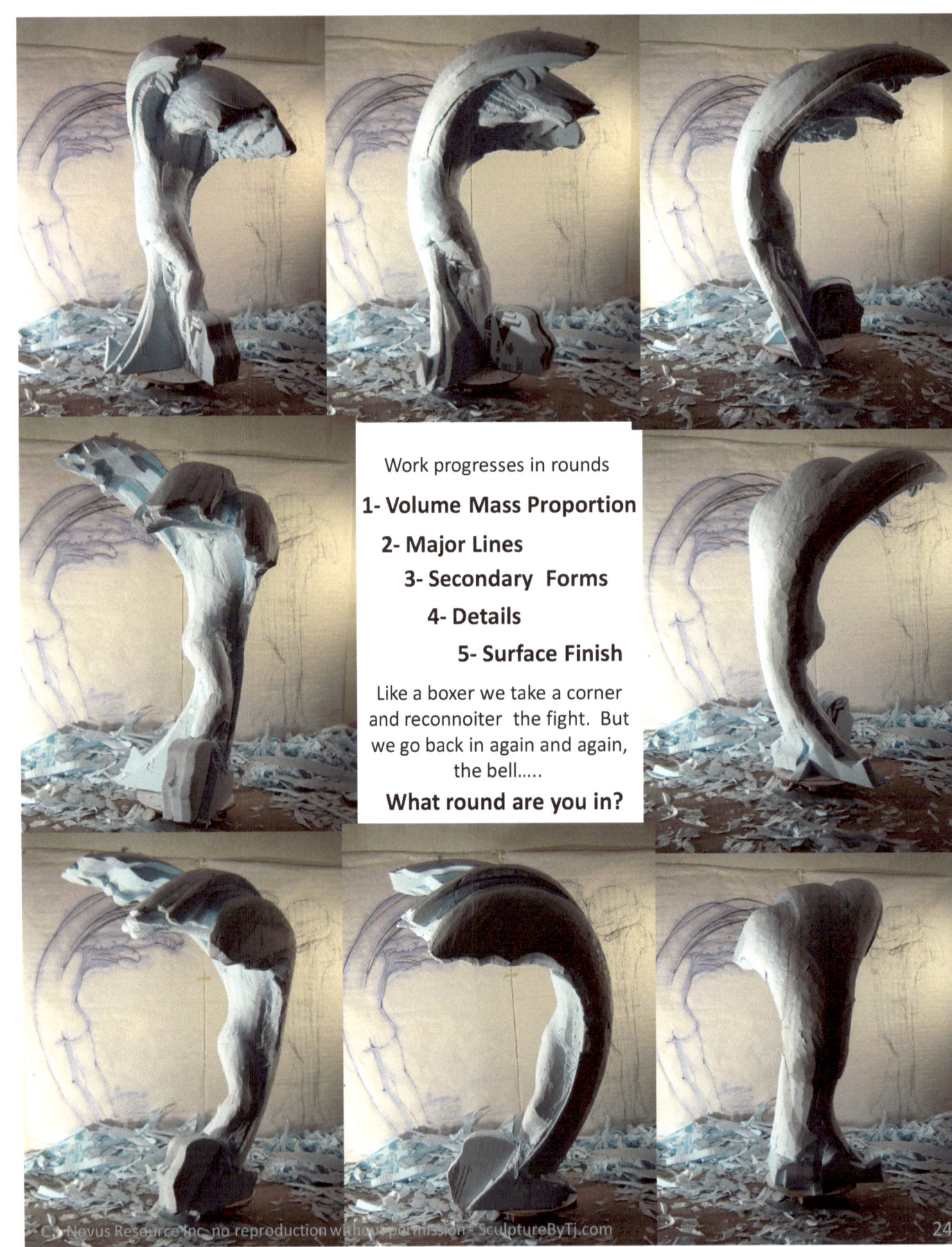

Work progresses in rounds

1- Volume Mass Proportion

2- Major Lines

3- Secondary Forms

4- Details

5- Surface Finish

Like a boxer we take a corner and reconnoiter the fight. But we go back in again and again, the bell.....

What round are you in?

Fixing Errors and Oversights

If you suspect you may be short of material it is a good idea to leave a flat area un-carved. This enables easily adding on another plank. Here you can see I decided to add to both edges of the major arm appendage. One of these was cut too short and I didn't spot it before attaching. Solution? Use the plastic to template the area, and add another piece.

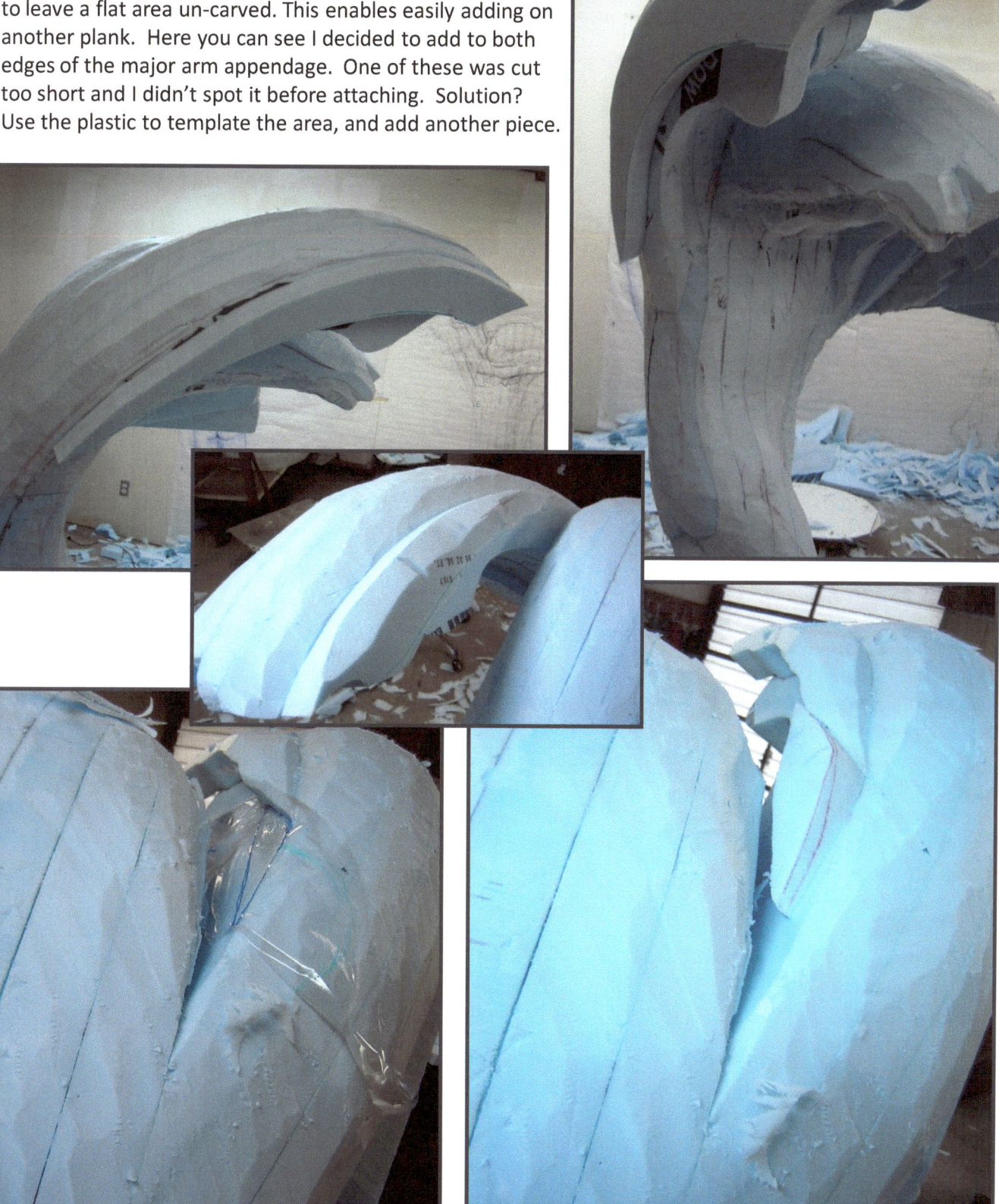

More Additions

To make a good joint I carved away a bit of material at the top of this repair area and flattened off the foam.

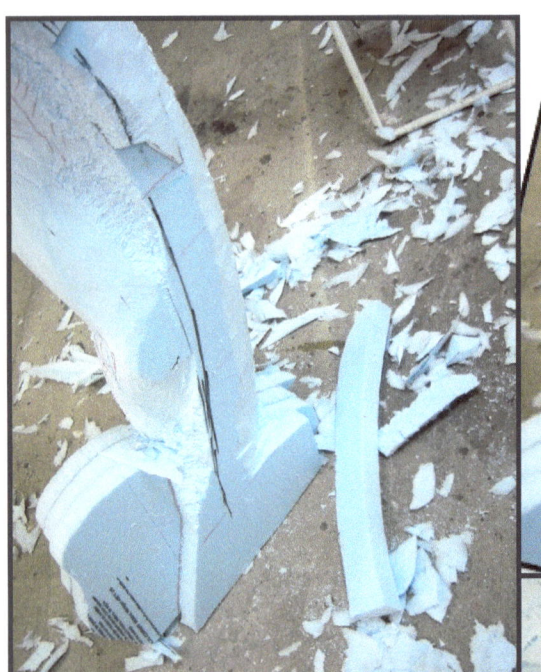

Then I cut a piece to match the area and glued it in.

The long arm form up under the extended appendage was not well planned. There was not enough material to carve the arm. In a tight place like this it is also difficult to carve easily. The solution was to make separate pieces and glue them in. The area was not flat however and I would have to cut the new piece to match the curve of the B&C planks. This is done by using a cardboard or foam core template to match up the mating surfaces.

Additions

Two pieces fitted to this surface and glued together create the stock blank for this arm. 1. (first piece pictured) This form was worked separately and left unattached and pinned in place with T pins. I decided to do a hand in similar fashion for the convenience of working detail.   All the forms around the arm and hand could now be carved easily.   This really helps in a tight area where you need to carve out negative space around detail.

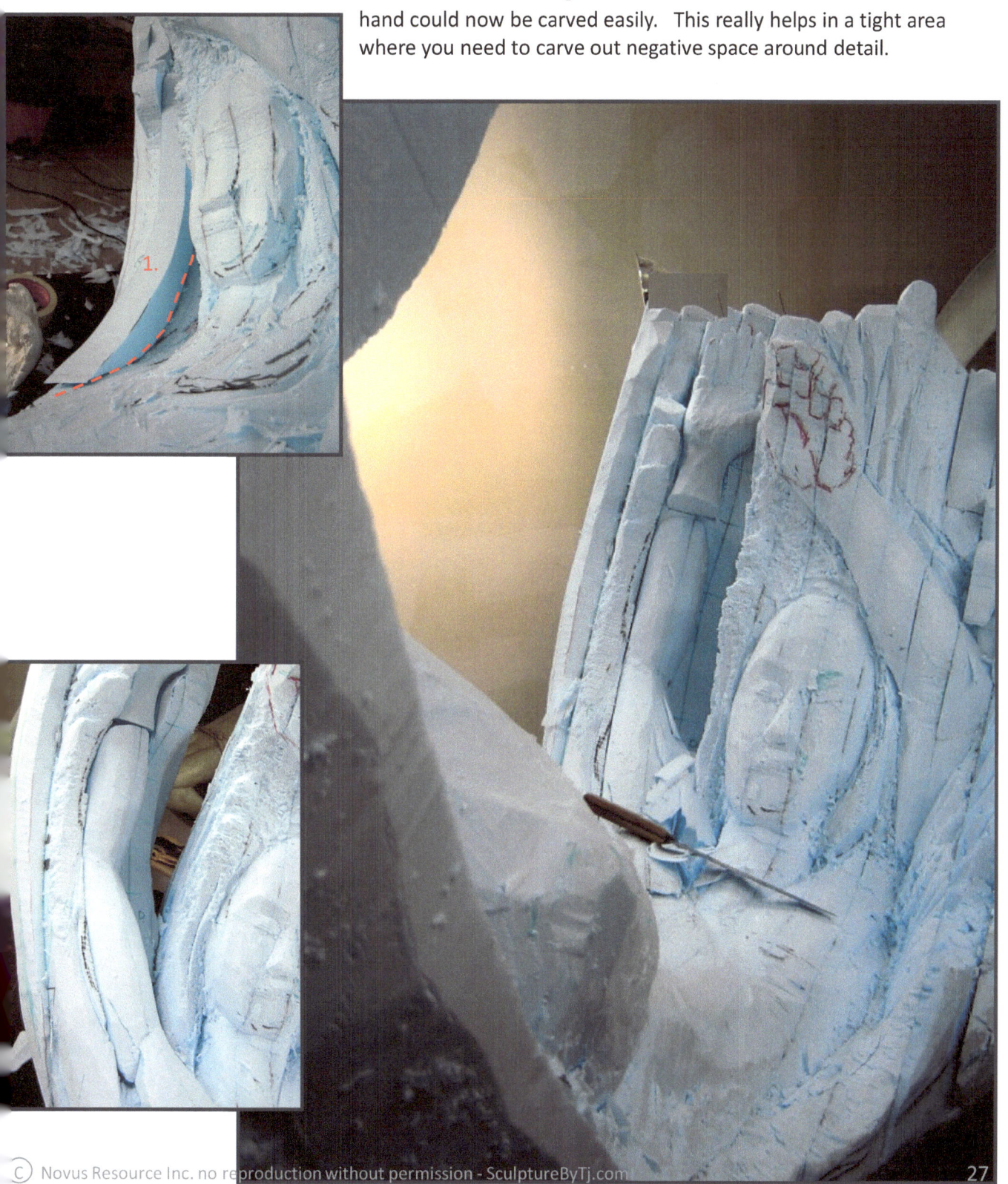

Carving Detail

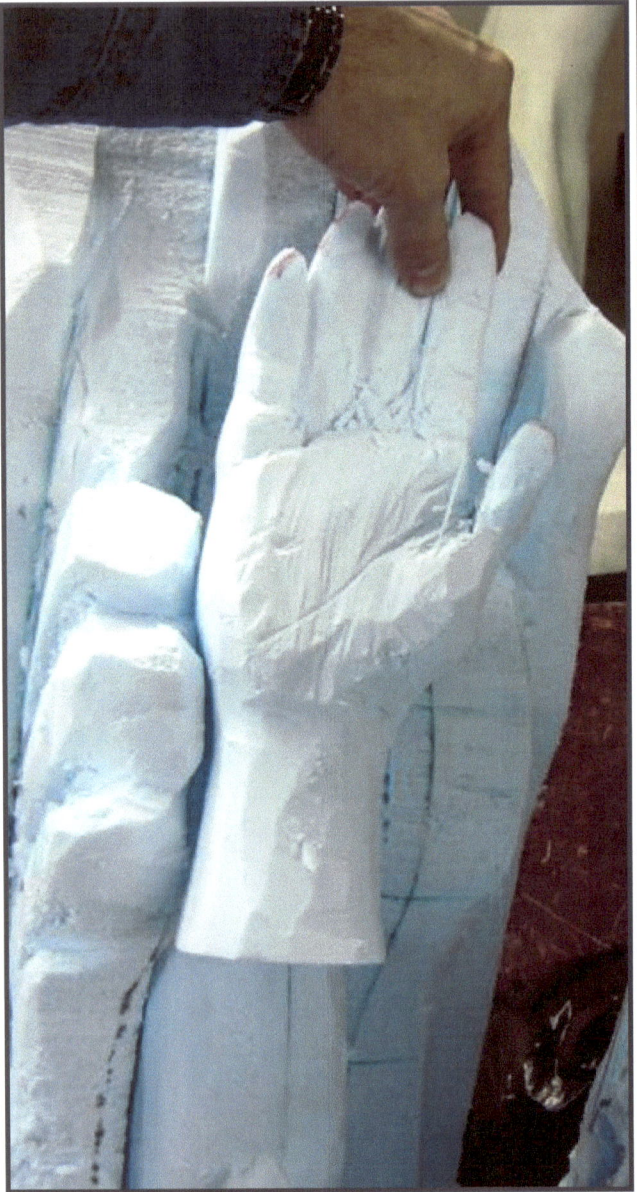

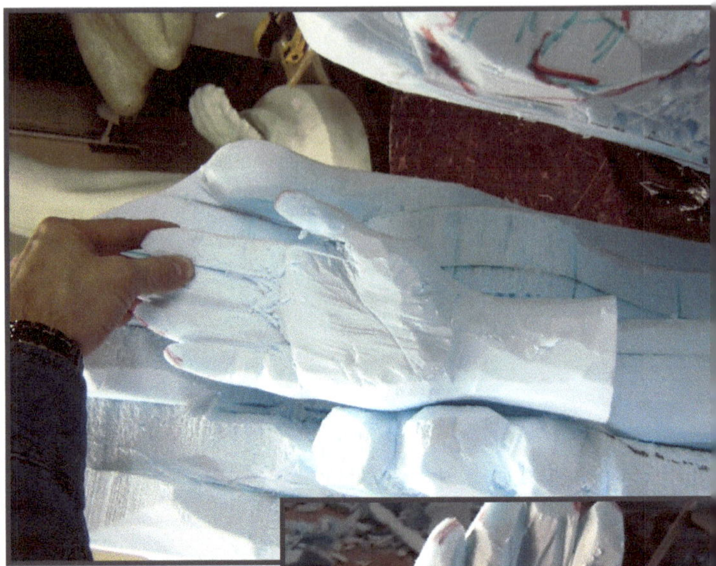

Carving requires clear knowledge of where you want the surface to be. Drawing on the foam and cutting carefully to edges and cleavages will get you fine results.

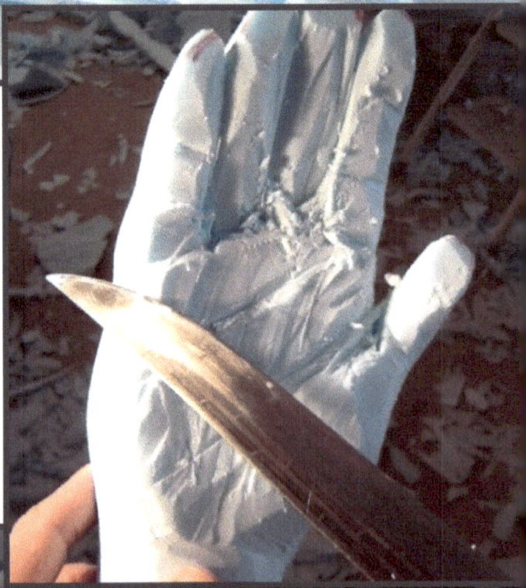

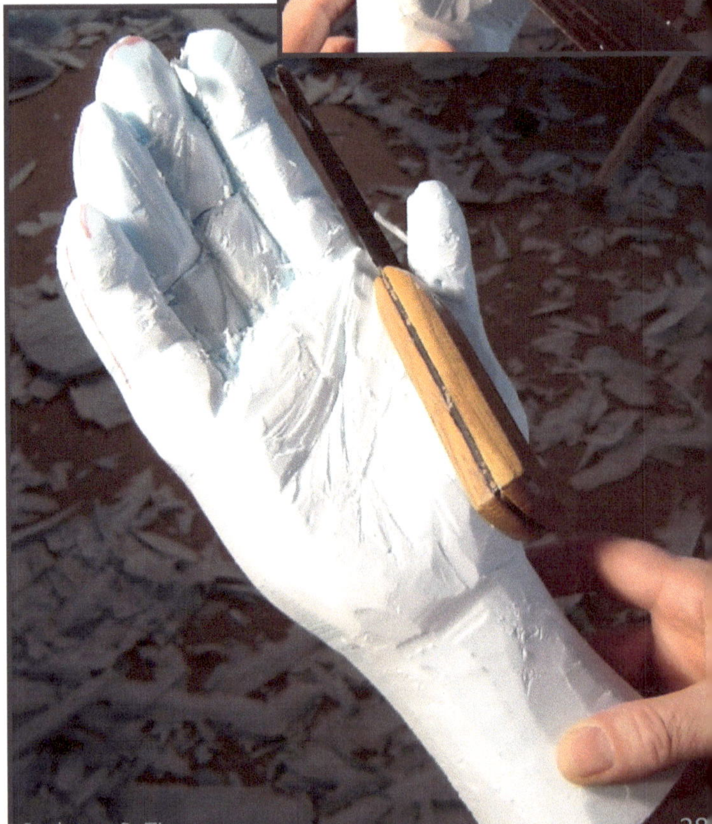

This hand was laid out and cut from a flat plank. The area it will be put in has to be hogged out to drop it in between the splashing forms. The back is left flat and sidesare trimmed until it drops in the cavity nicely. Then it is left loose to be able to refine it and surrounding details.

The hand pictured here was done with only the butcher knife. The curved tip on the knife allows some pretty agile maneuvers and even a hollow is doable with some practice.

Piecing in Intricate Detail Areas

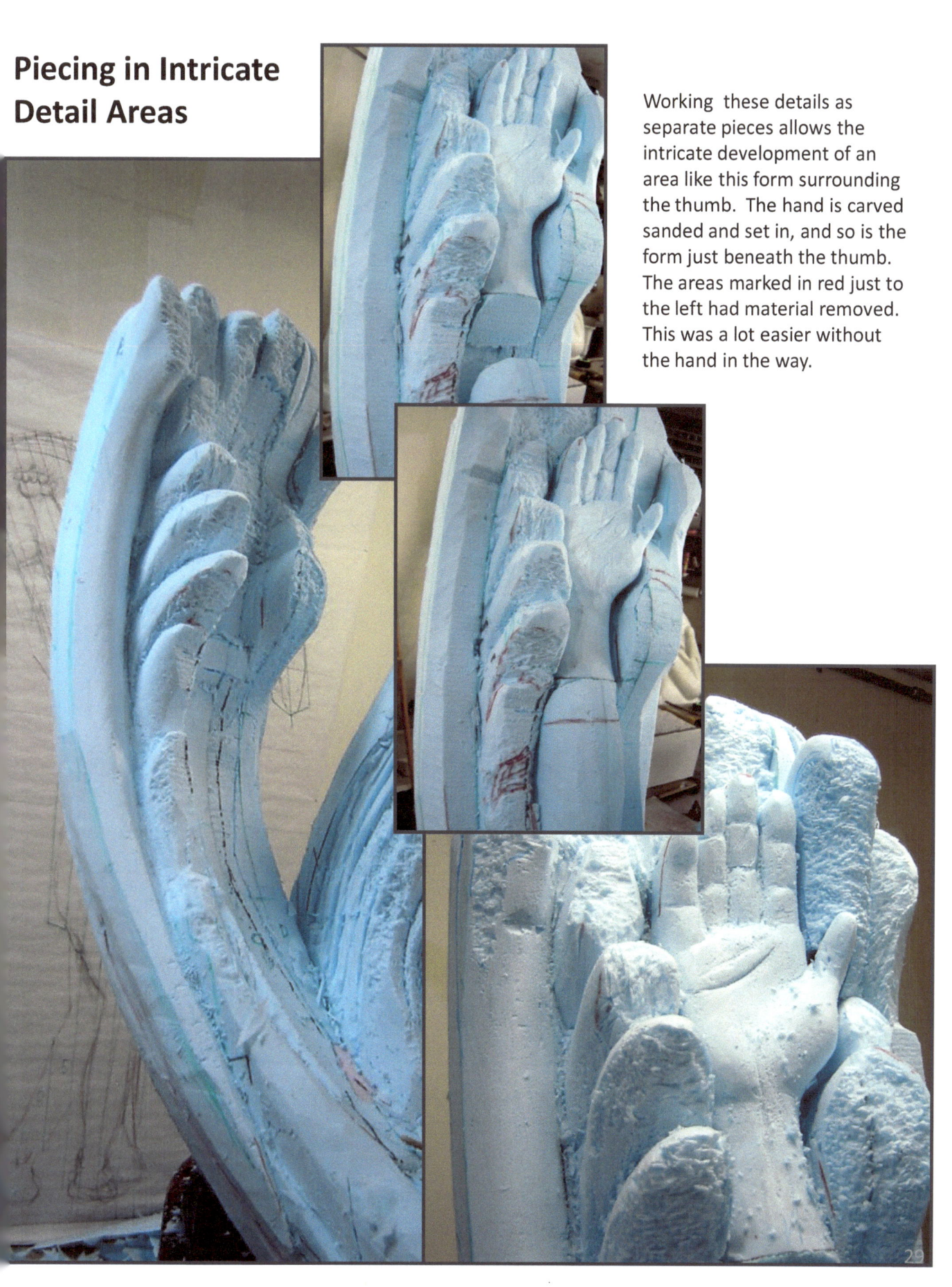

Working these details as separate pieces allows the intricate development of an area like this form surrounding the thumb. The hand is carved sanded and set in, and so is the form just beneath the thumb. The areas marked in red just to the left had material removed. This was a lot easier without the hand in the way.

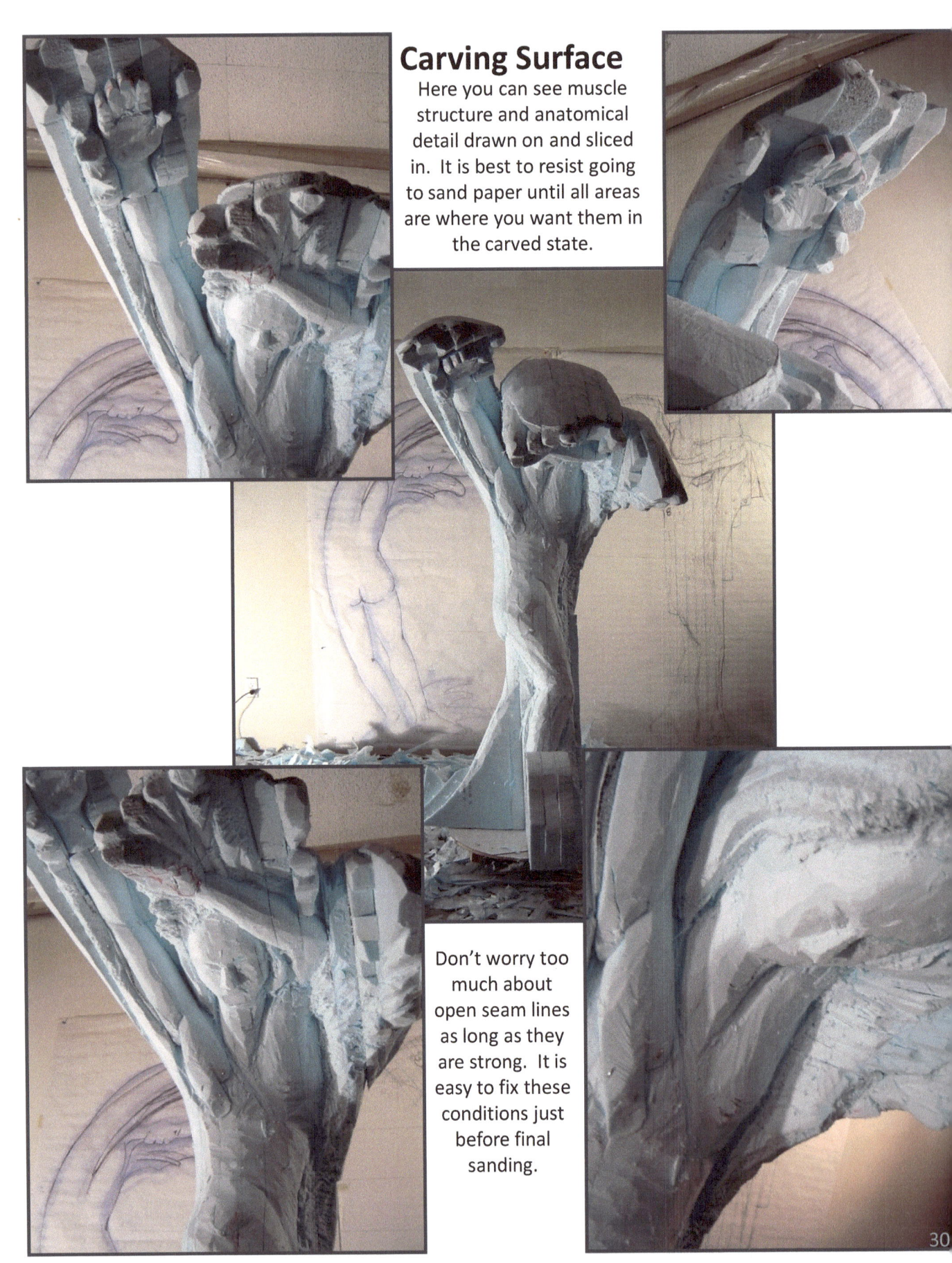

Carving Surface

Here you can see muscle structure and anatomical detail drawn on and sliced in. It is best to resist going to sand paper until all areas are where you want them in the carved state.

Don't worry too much about open seam lines as long as they are strong. It is easy to fix these conditions just before final sanding.

Detail Additions

In this area there was a need for more material to make curling forms. I cut pieces and matched them to the existing areas, sometimes carving and flattening the base or back area to make a better seam. You can do as much or as little to the loose piece before gluing.

Reworking

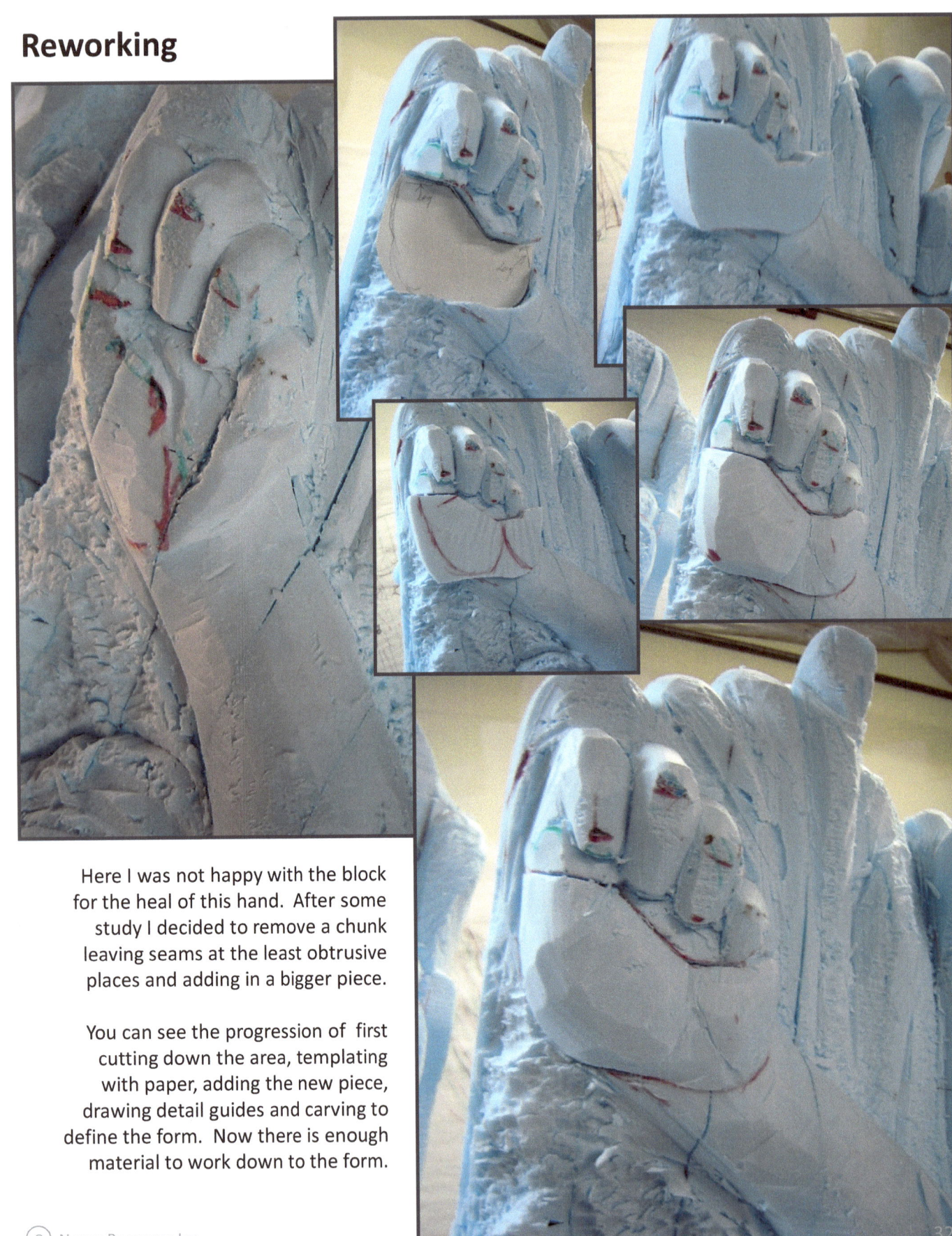

Here I was not happy with the block for the heal of this hand. After some study I decided to remove a chunk leaving seams at the least obtrusive places and adding in a bigger piece.

You can see the progression of first cutting down the area, templating with paper, adding the new piece, drawing detail guides and carving to define the form. Now there is enough material to work down to the form.

Solidifying a Joint

This joint was not solid and I was concerned that it would be too weak, causing trouble later. The solution was 5 minute epoxy.

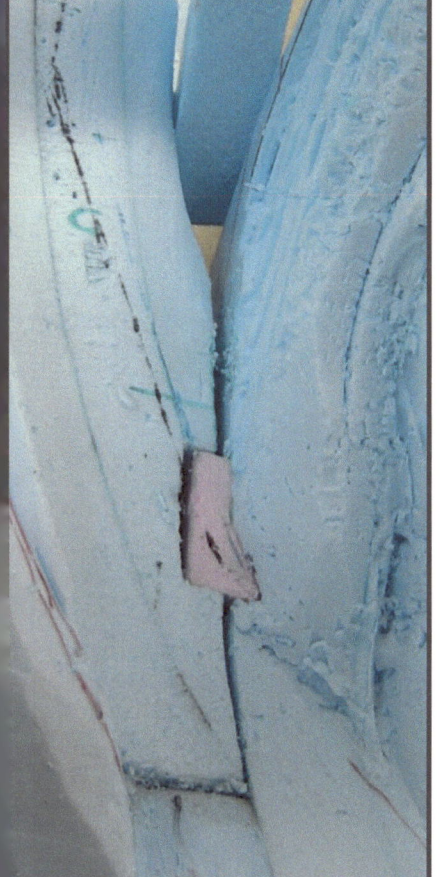

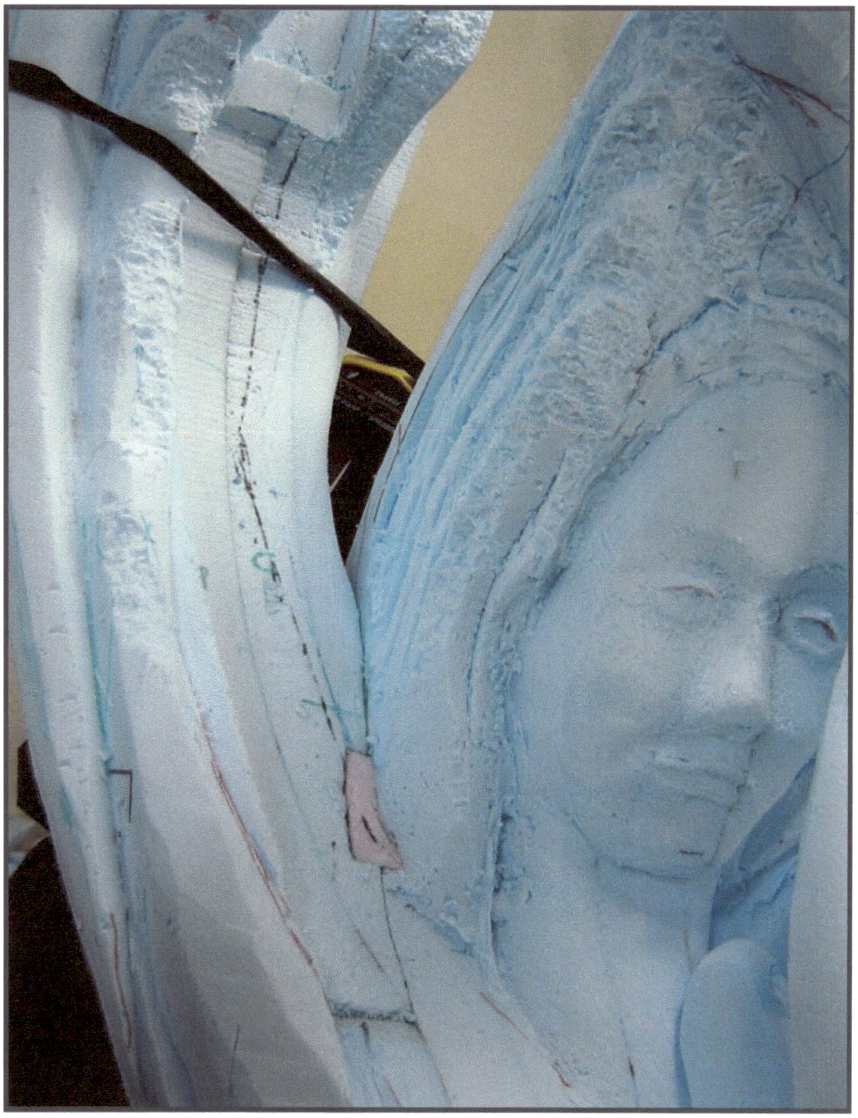

I'd done enough carving to know that hard material in this intersection will not be in the path. I spread it out, and poured in the epoxy. Some times getting a clamp on a form takes some inventive methods. The rubber band is a piece of inner tube. This pulls the appendage over until the glue sets.

Now this critical joint seems solid. I left this operation until I knew I would not be carving into the glue.

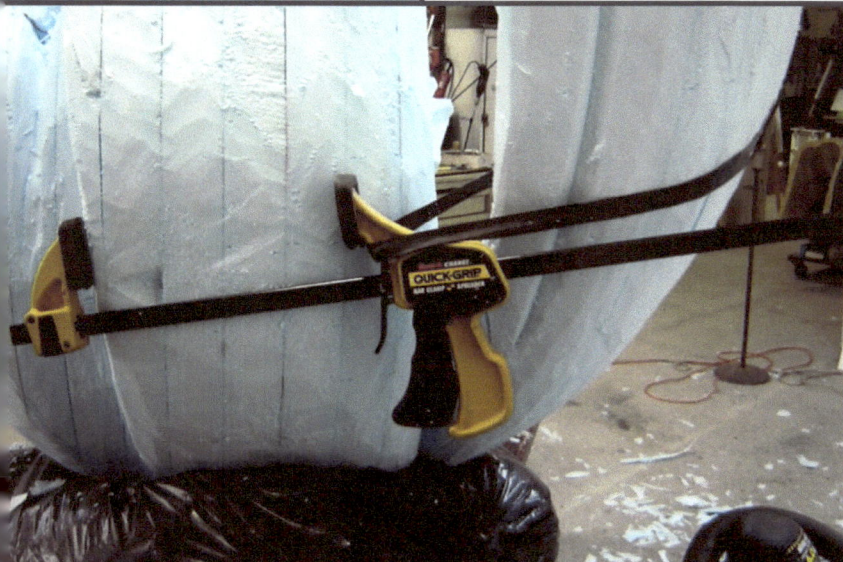

** Alas, this was not the end of the story of this joint, see the addendum.

Turning to the Big Piece

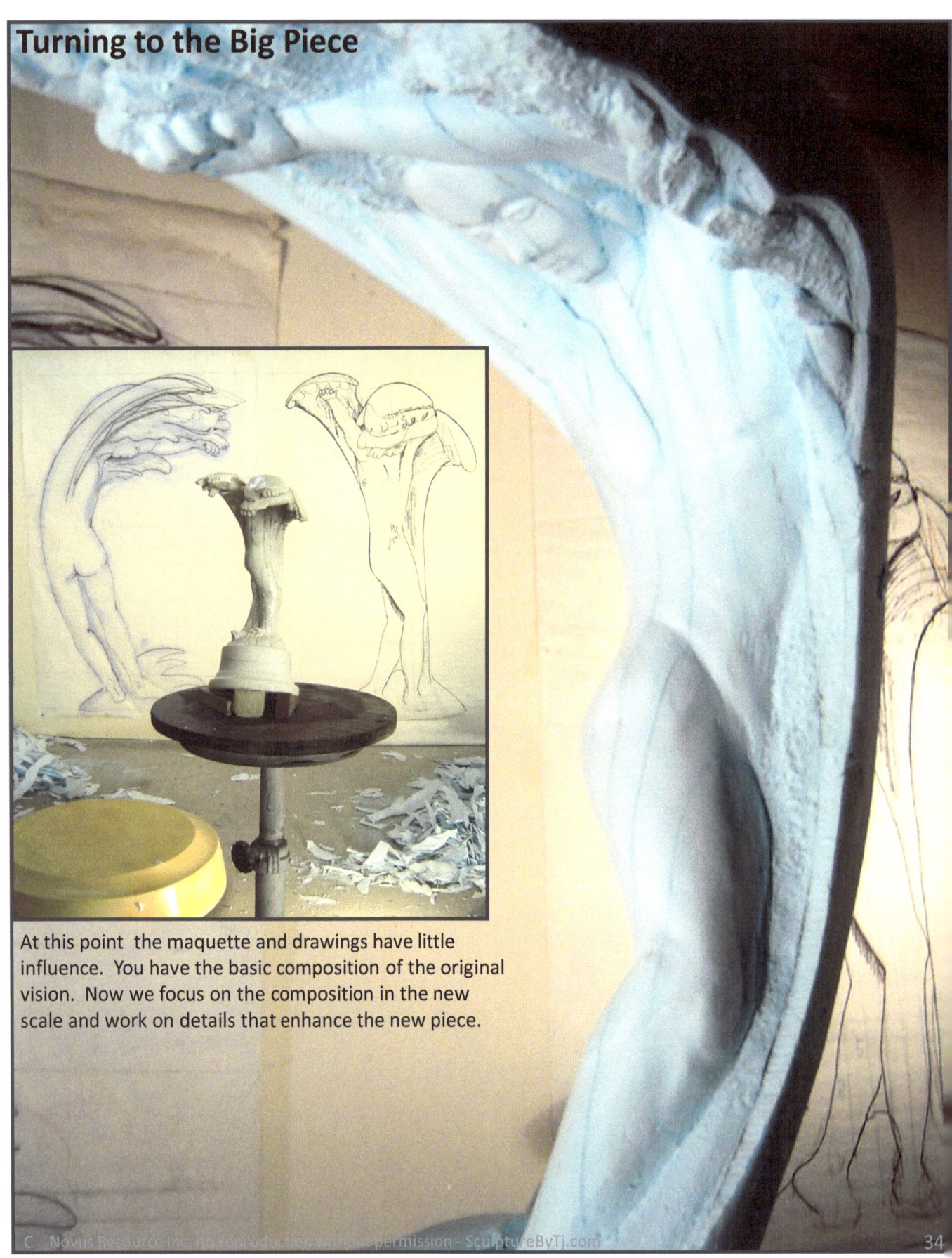

At this point the maquette and drawings have little influence. You have the basic composition of the original vision. Now we focus on the composition in the new scale and work on details that enhance the new piece.

Funky Area?   No Problem- Replace it!

This breast muscle was a place where I was just not happy with the fit of pieces. There was a flap of loose stuff and it wasn't really high enough to just carve down. The solution was to cut out the area and flatten a space for a new piece. Here you see two nice straight cut lines on a paper template, to define the new piece. Next shot has a fitted piece, and then a shot of the finished area.

Key to this type of repair is good straight lines at the joints and a flat surface down in the bottom to glue to.

Once it gets carved off and sanded the seam is of little consequence, especially with the stone coat finish.

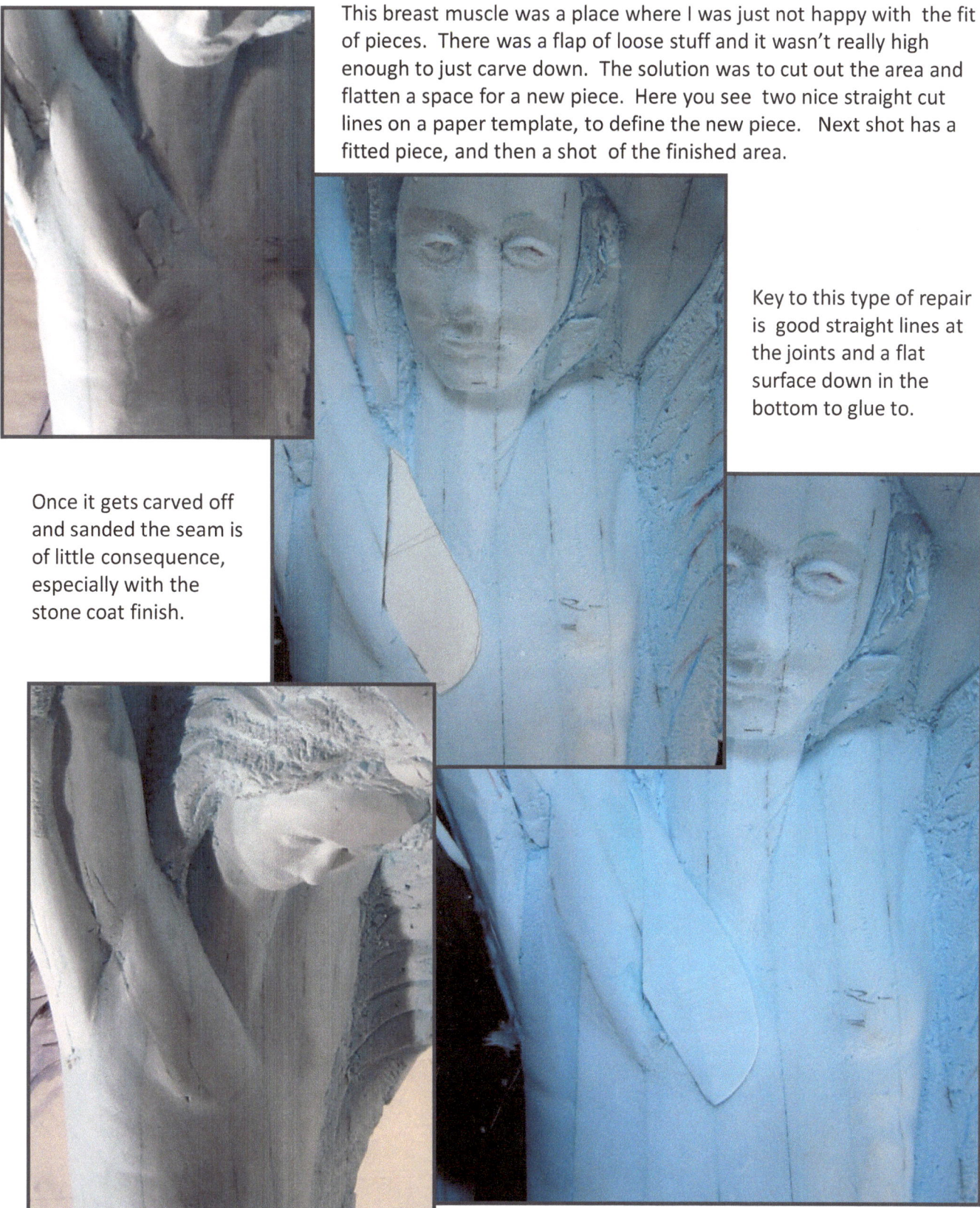

Round 5
Surface Finish
Before Sanding

Now the sanding process can begin on the interior details. These are unlikely to get dented as you fixture the piece.

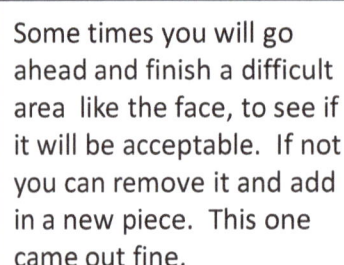

Some times you will go ahead and finish a difficult area like the face, to see if it will be acceptable. If not you can remove it and add in a new piece. This one came out fine.

Once you sand a surface down you have to protect it from denting until you put a hard coating on it. The back of this form is left until last since It will be placed on the bench frequently.

Completing the Base

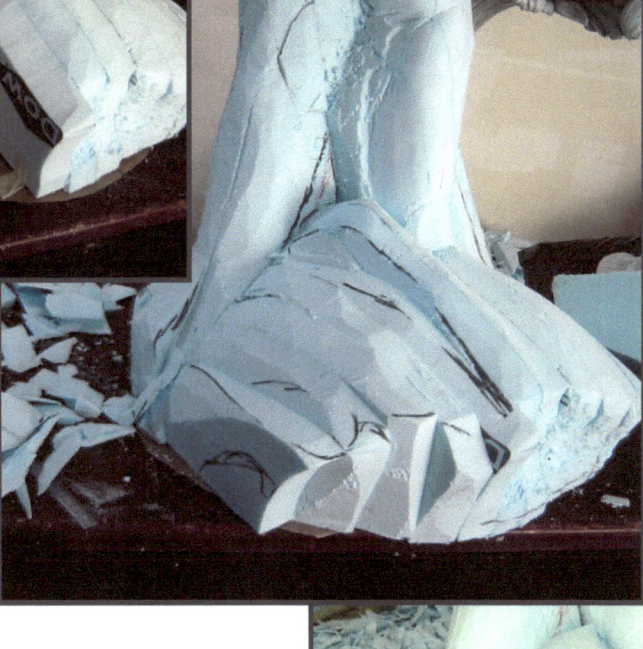

Now all the upper forms are where we want them. It is time to complete the composition down at the base. I wanted to be roughly within the circle of this display pedestal, but the work needed to be done on the bench, and not on the pedestal itself. I traced a circle on paper and fastened it to the piece as a guide. This allows placing pieces and fleshing out the base area. Pieces are added to make a block to work with.

A review of the maquette and some new thinking on the composition on this larger scale produced some concepts for the new form. Here we're marking and designing as the pieces are placed.

The light weight of this material allows you to lift it up onto the work bench for easier carving of the lower section. The work is constantly moving from bench to reviewing turntable to get all the perspectives as you carve. But foam is easy to lift. "Hey, watch that ceiling fan!"

Patch Pieces & Problems

Here is what can happen when you rush. I was being called away when I sprayed too thick a coat of 77 on these pieces. It could have been OK but I pushed them together too early. The solvent doesn't flash off in a closed space, instead it continues to dissolve foam! I was able to re-sand and glue this piece back in.

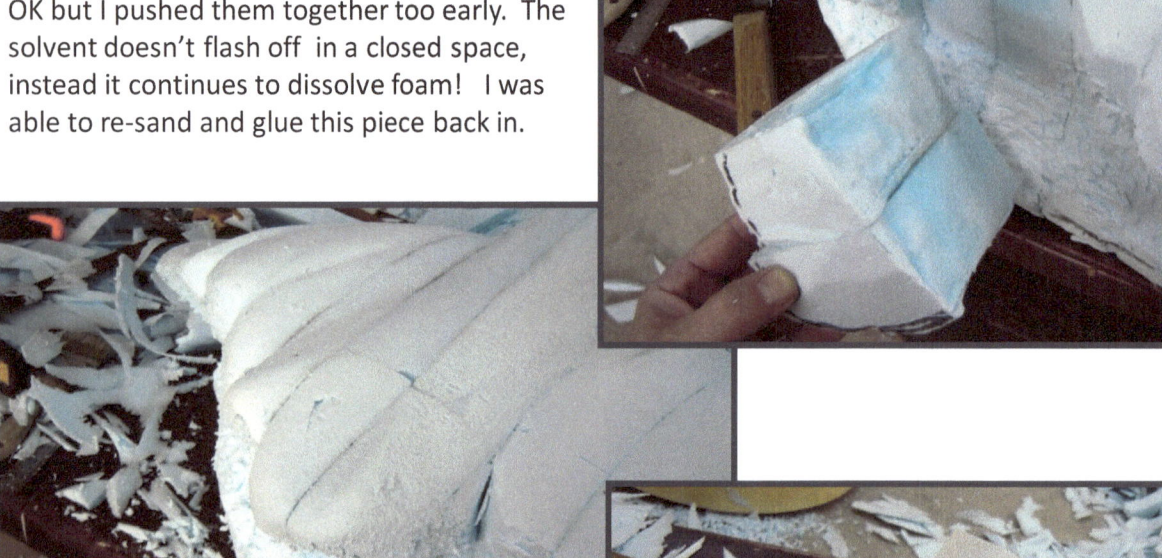

A good trick for when you need to add in a piece is the old "hole in the paper" trick to mask for spraying glue. Below is the inserted piece.

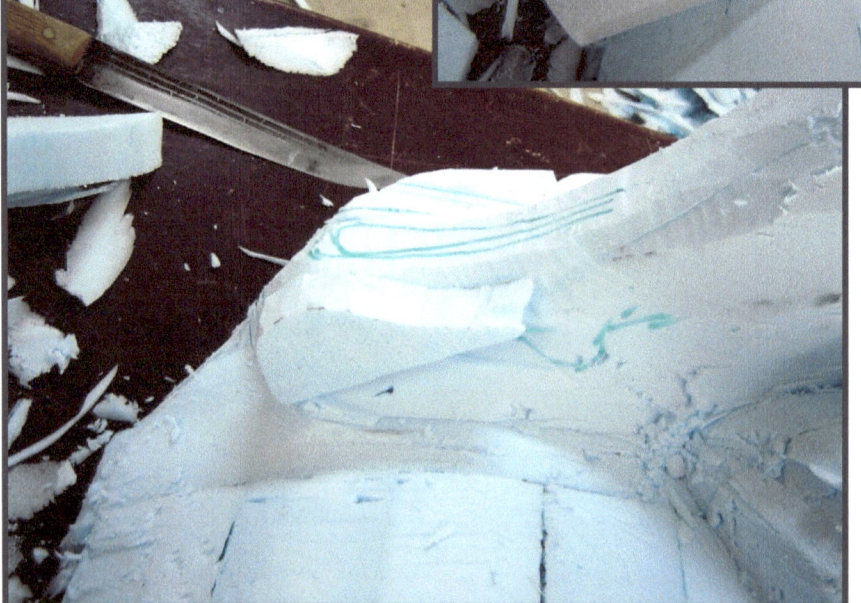

Be sure to dispose of the glue mask paper properly because they can be very unsightly stuck to your shoe.

Ready for Finish Sanding?

The extent to which you tune the surface is dependant on the finish technique and coatings that you will use at the end. If you are going to spray plastic or use the drywall mud then very careful attention is required here. If you are using the Stone Coating cement you need not worry about scratch marks, only the form of the surface and the contours are important. A bell should go off when you switch processes, and you should reflect on the entire project before the commitment.

Choosing From Finishing Processes

There are many ways to use a carved foam piece. It can be a pattern or model from which you pull a mold and then cast a piece. It can be the finished piece if it is short term and for indoor use. Or you can put a hard coating that will make it fairly durable for good indoor use and even some outdoor applications.

Pattern and Mold- You can pull a plaster or **hydrocal mold** from the foam just the way it is with a simple greasing of Vaseline. Brush it, rub it in with your hands and smear it on all surfaces and plaster will pull away easily. Concrete forms can be made this way. Small imperfections can be sanded out of the mold. Industrial **modeling clays,** like those available from Chevant Clay, and **waxes** from foundry supply sources can be applied over the foam for better detail and different texture techniques.

Drywall mud is a fast finishing option If you are going for a refined pattern with intricate detail. I use **Durabond** brand fast dry. This material can be mixed in small batches and painted on the surface in any thickness. You can alter the consistency to suit your detail needs. A very smooth finish can be produced with this material. Just know that your pattern will be a "one time use" tool. To allow perfect sanding you can add microbaloons to the Durabond which will make this material very close to the density of foam. This will let you sand both foam and patched areas with little distortion due to density difference. Microbaloons are an additive for resins used in boat manufacture, available from fiberglass and concrete industrial supply houses. Durabond can be sprayed on with a gravity gun or drywall hopper gun used by contractors.

Plaster or Hydrocal are other options for this type of model. These can be painted on , sprayed and worked via the usual tools. When you break through a thin coat you will have to take away foam and patch with more plaster. The hardness difference prevents easy sanding. In both these cases you will want to seal the model with shellac when you are all done before making any type of mold. Plaster of course can be painted but it is not a very durable finish.

Indoor Use- film props/ display pieces You can coat it with various materials to harden the surface. **5 minute epoxy** can be thinned with alcohol and used as a coating. Smooth On makes a spray system that is good for props but the spray equipment will cost you. Various **epoxies** can be purchased but beware the allergy and health risks to these industrial products.

Medium Range Use- architectural ornament (even outdoor sculpture) For a medium life span you can coat it with **Stone Coat polymer-modified cement** which produces a very hard surface that is quite durable and even stabile for some outdoor use, depending on thickness. The basic materials are used for floors, walls and stucco finish. My formula has fiberglass that makes it strong and micro fiber that makes it very resistant to surface cracking and offers the ability to grind and polish for a nice stone-like effect. Many options for pigmentation, aggregate inclusion, and staining allow elegant artistic work. I have gravitated to this material for its beauty and durability. (And of course you can always take a mold from this as well). The draw back is the surface work. It must be applied more thickly, and troweled to get a finished surface. Once set this stuff is hard as rock and requires a lot of effort to sand and work surfaces. All this means careful and time consuming application compared to Durabond, plaster, epoxy or sprayed plastic.

Sanding - Now you eat dust while you dial in the surface

Once you get into sand paper be prepared for the dust. The particles are light and cling with static so you need a vacuum at the ready to deal with the mess. Of course, use a particle mask. This stuff will catch in your throat and make you uncomfortable. I keep my shop vac near by and use an assortment of very soft brushes to dust the piece and the tools as I work. A button-down dress shirt and a shop apron keep the dust off me. Sanding requires an extremely delicate pressure and total awareness of any contact with the work to prevent marks and gouges. You will need to practice to get complex forms. Fingers behind sand paper leave grooves; use a board or block. ***Always cross hatch*** your strokes with all tools! Grooves are created instantly with one stroke. Evenly rotate sanding tubes used in crevasses and side walls need to be cross hatched.

Large surfaces need a large board. I find my body sander with some 36 grit is OK for a start but you must stroke lightly and not apply much pressure or foam will tear. You will quickly want to go to 100 grit and then to 180.

If there is too much material, grab the blade and slice off a bit before going back to the paper. There is a slight grain to this material and there can also be an orientation to fresh sand paper grains. If it starts to tear you may want to stroke differently.

A light touch is a must. If you bear down it stretches the foam and tears. Let the grits do the cutting. Work down in the crevasses first and then up over high areas. Often, just a small piece of sand paper folded into a shape that gets into your form is the trick. But watch out for corners. Sand paper corners that curl can leave a gouge just when you thought you were done. Glued to a board or tool is better. Occasionally a fine rasp can help in tight areas, but stroke lightly.

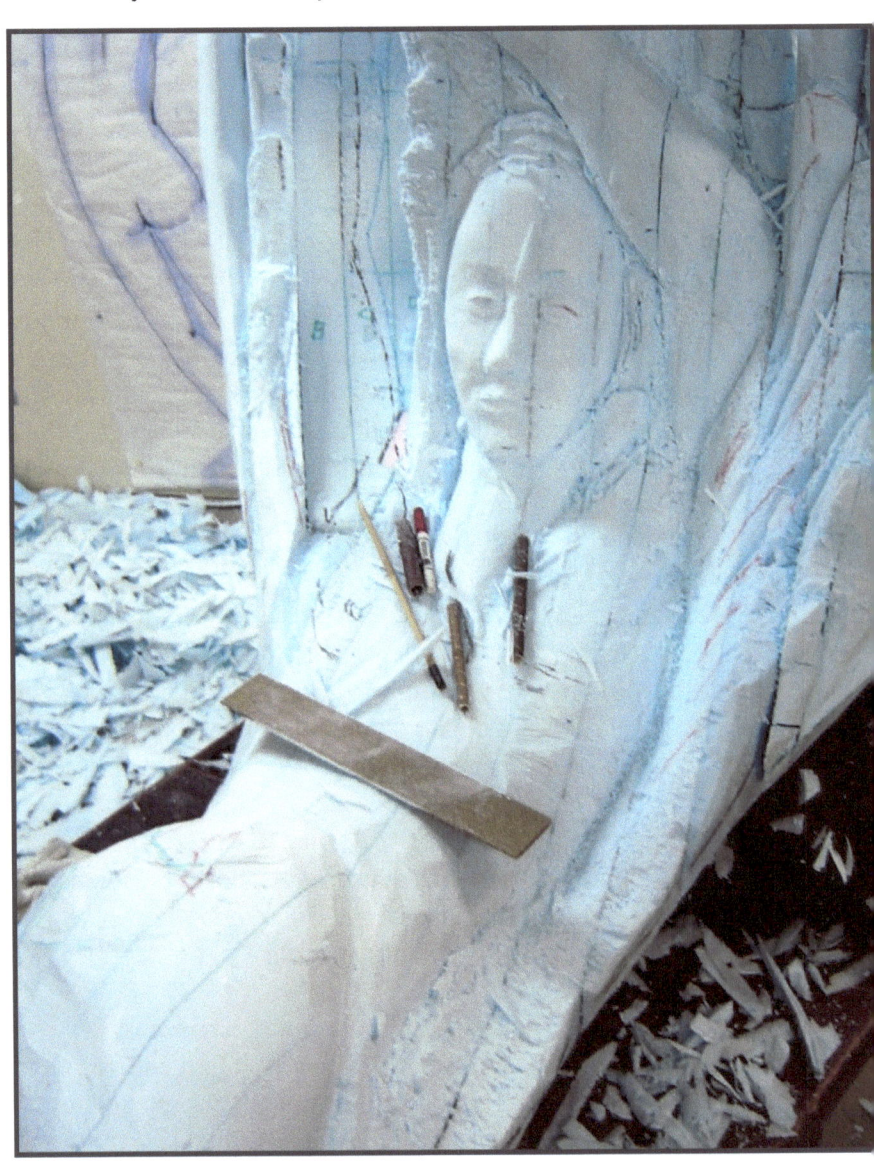

Approach sanding the same way as carving. Define high points with light markings so you don't take them off.

Sanding

Here you can see the before and after views of the figure's surfaces. They were sanded with about 100 grit sand paper. Making tools with spray 77 and masonite that have various edge profiles really helps get in the tight areas. For stone coating I probably went overboard on the fine grit but it is hard to resist finishing well. "Uh, just a helpful practice exercise in anatomical study that we will use in the final coat?" That's a good excuse.

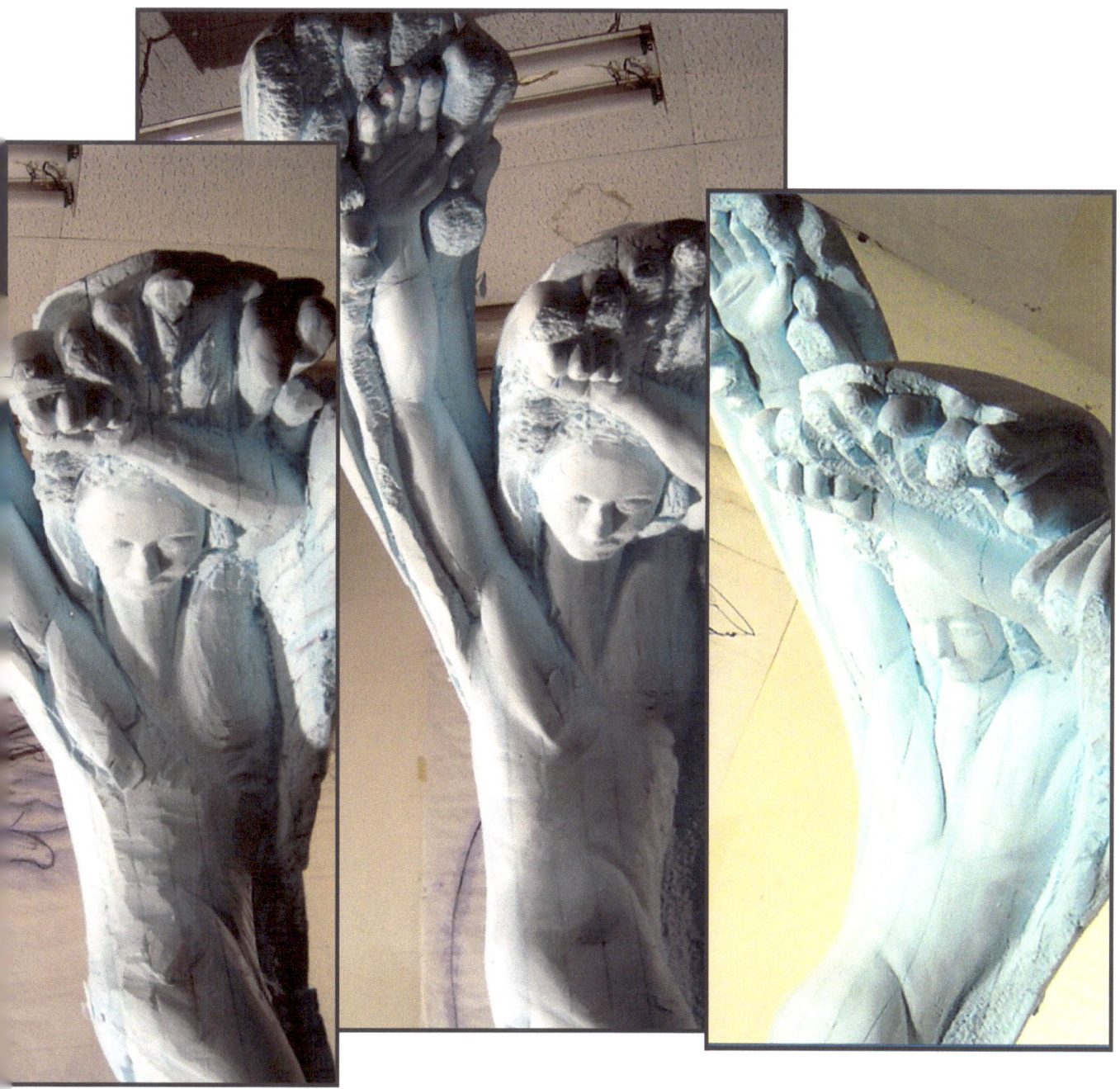

Got Gaps?

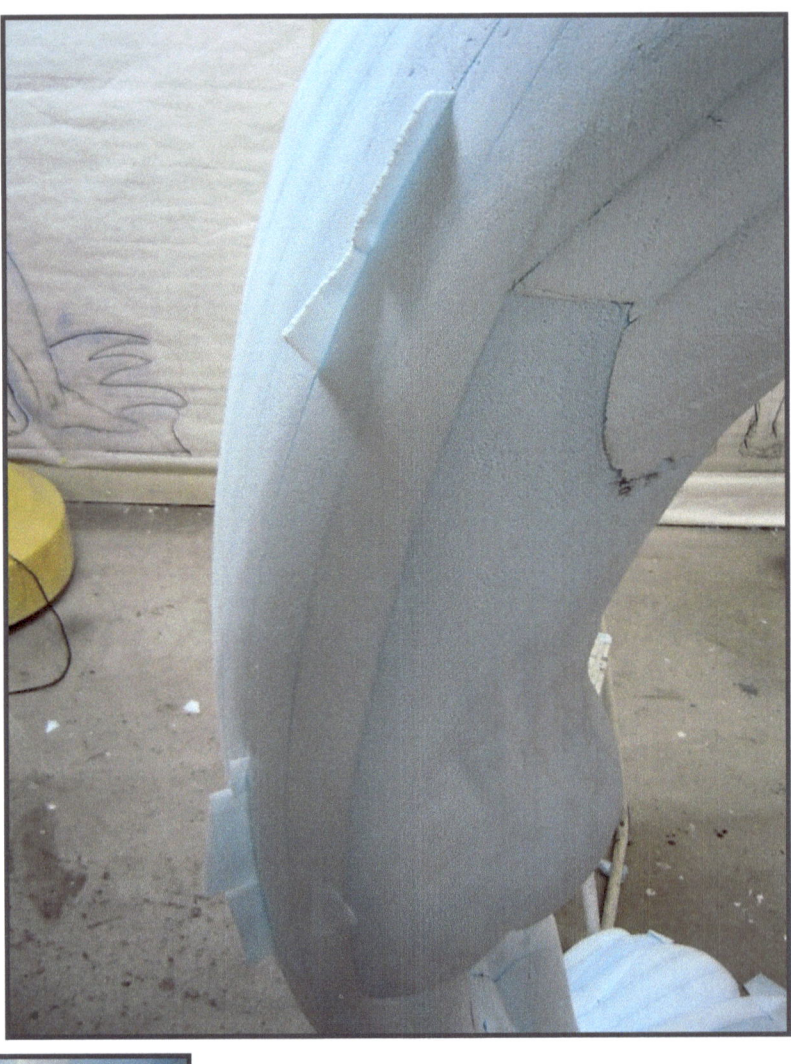

And all those gaps between planks and gouges or unfinished places? Now is when you fix these. It is unbelievably simple. You pick up those pieces from the floor and slice thin wedges to jamb into the cracks. If need be, you can slice these on the band saw but it doesn't take much to fill gaps. In many cases you don't even need glue! Just wedge them in and slice sideways with your sharp blade. A stroke of sand paper and the crack disappears.

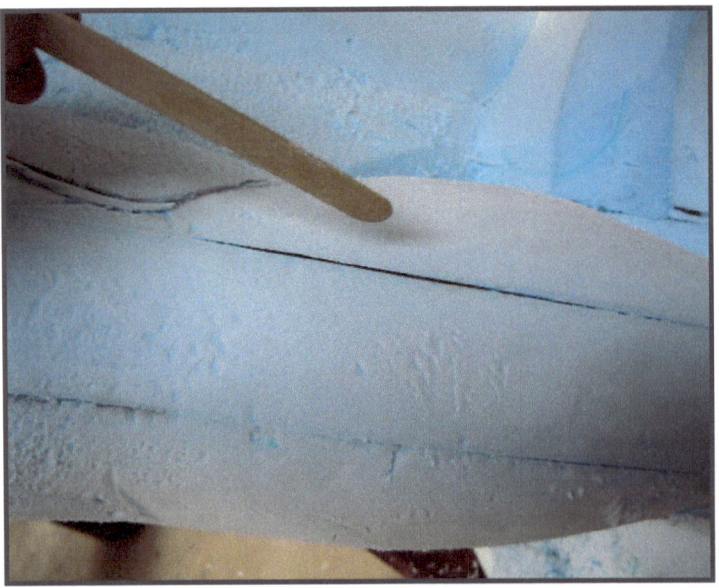

The same is true for a joint that didn't stick well. Here you slip in a tongue depressor sprayed with glue, let it tack up, and press the pieces together.

Fixing by Filling

Here is a large gap where the blocks did not get positioned correctly. A filler wedge is cut and fit. Spray 77 glue on a tongue depressor and wiped into the crevasse. Then stuff in the wedge and cut off the excess. These fixes pretty much disappear.

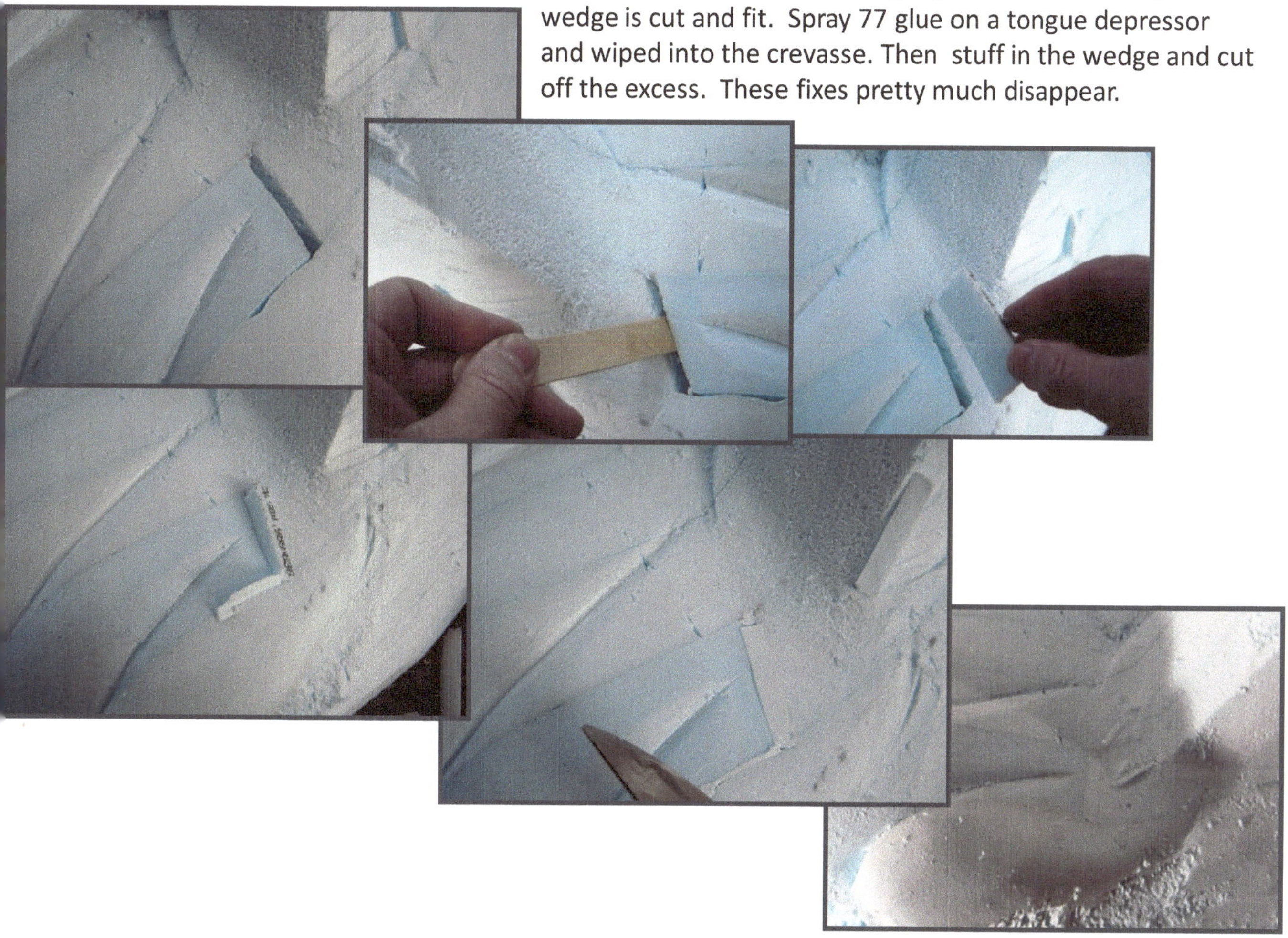

On the edge of the base where the blocks are just slightly short you add little chunks and carve back against the volume so as not to pull them out with the carving motion. At sanding stage these are not noticeable. Here you see gluing on the bench, carved and sanded on the pedestal and stone coat finish.

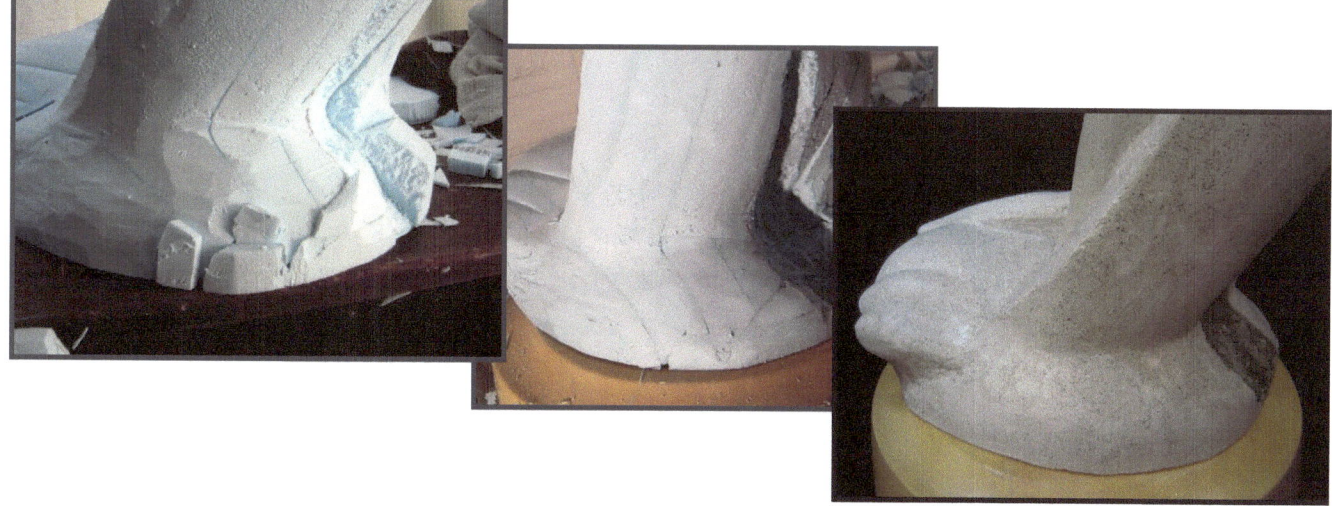

43

Final View

Now the piece is ready to coat. Some seams are still visible and a few details not complete.

Some detail, like muscle structure, has been left exaggerated so the final coating process doesn't hide it.

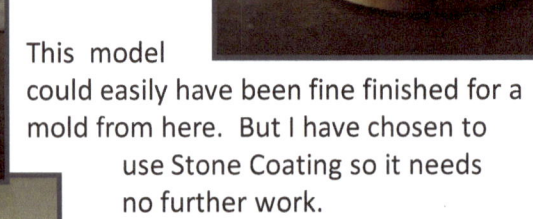

This model could easily have been fine finished for a mold from here. But I have chosen to use Stone Coating so it needs no further work.

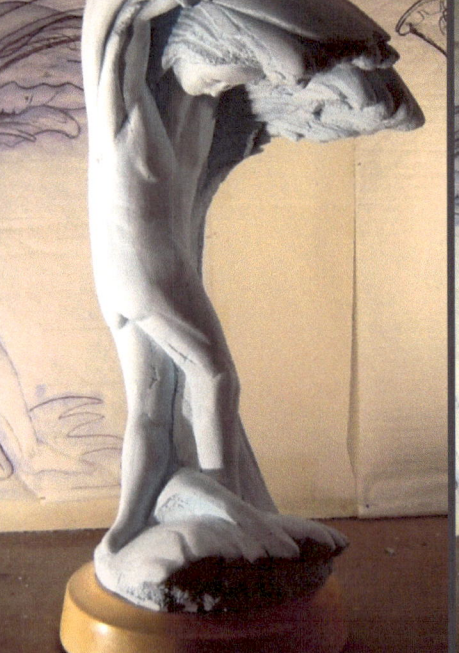

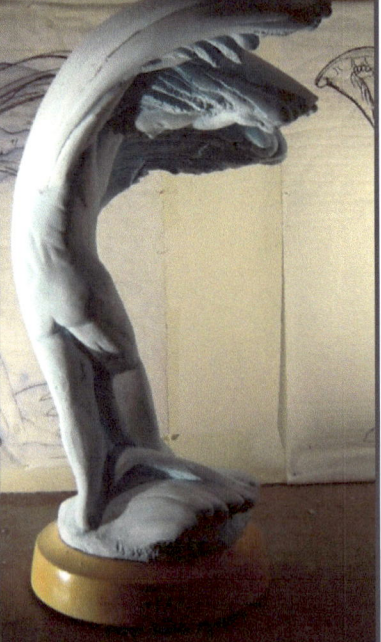

This level is fine for the finishing process that has been chosen. Ready for final coating.

Next Steps

You are ready to move on to *Book 3, Stone Coating*. Tj continues the visual story on this same piece and explains each operation as we work, with points about tools, materials and techniques. The final finish book *Stone Coating* offers a new method from modern materials that produce dramatic results.

Modern formulas for polymer modified cement, have been developed for the concrete countertop and architectural ornamentation fields. These formulas have been adapted, simplified, enhanced, and then illustrated for you in this volume. You will learn tricks known only to a handful of concrete professionals on how to create a light-weight, hard, durable, coating formula with artistic finishes that will last and last.

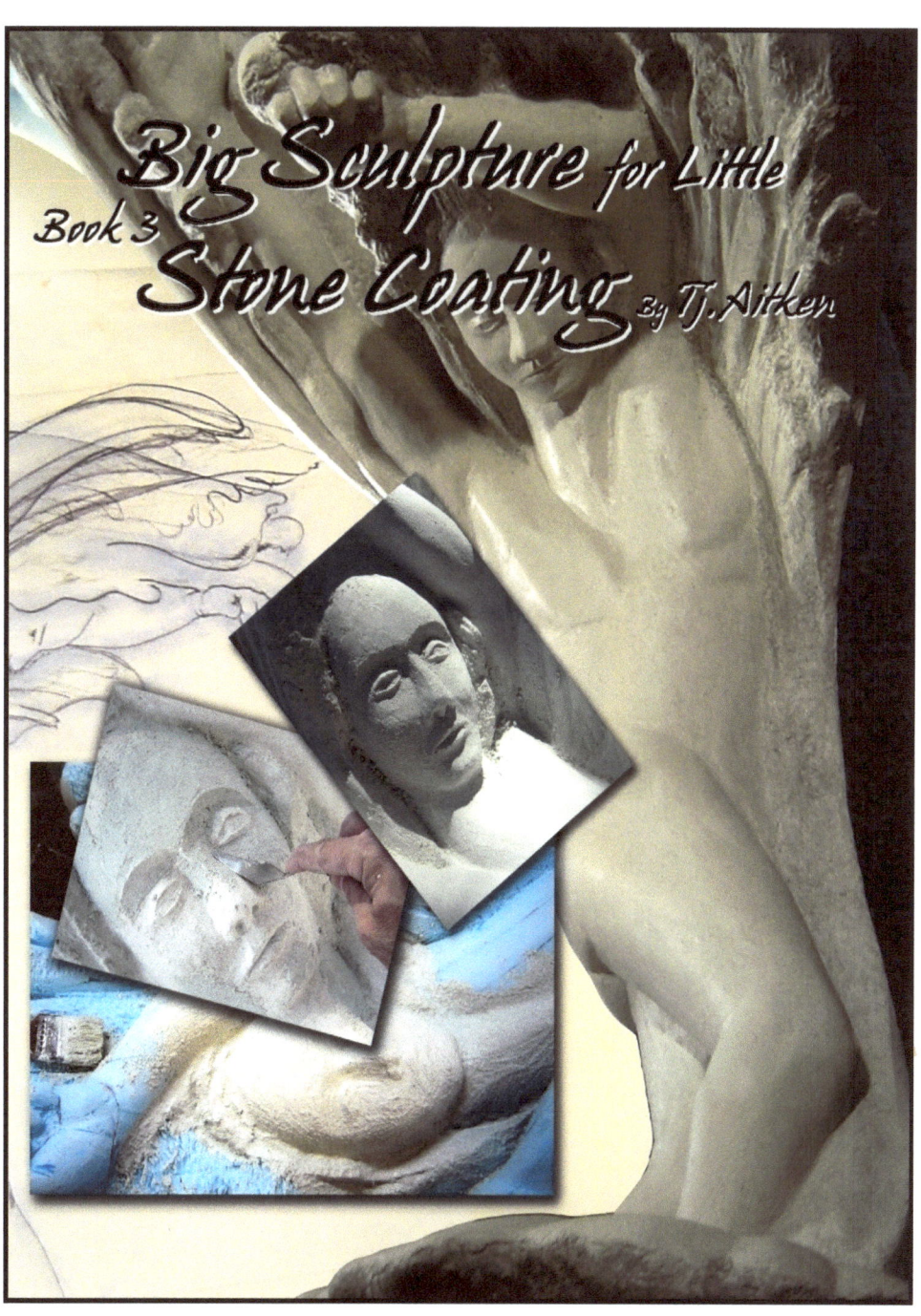

available at: **www.SculptureByTj.com**

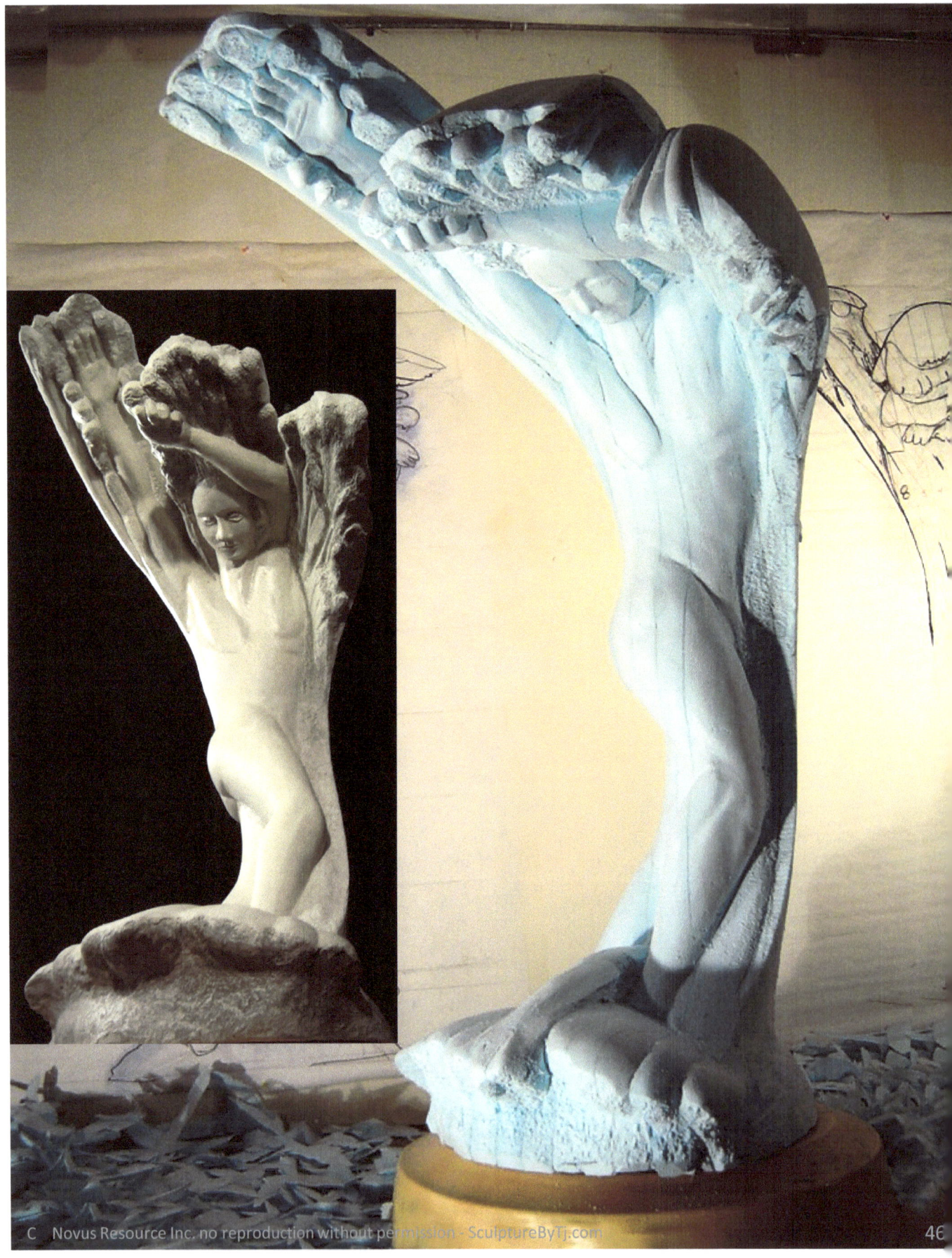

About the Art Work

Impacted Man is from an installation called ***Major Impact***. It has been under development since 1997 when a group of maquettes were done as studies for the piece.

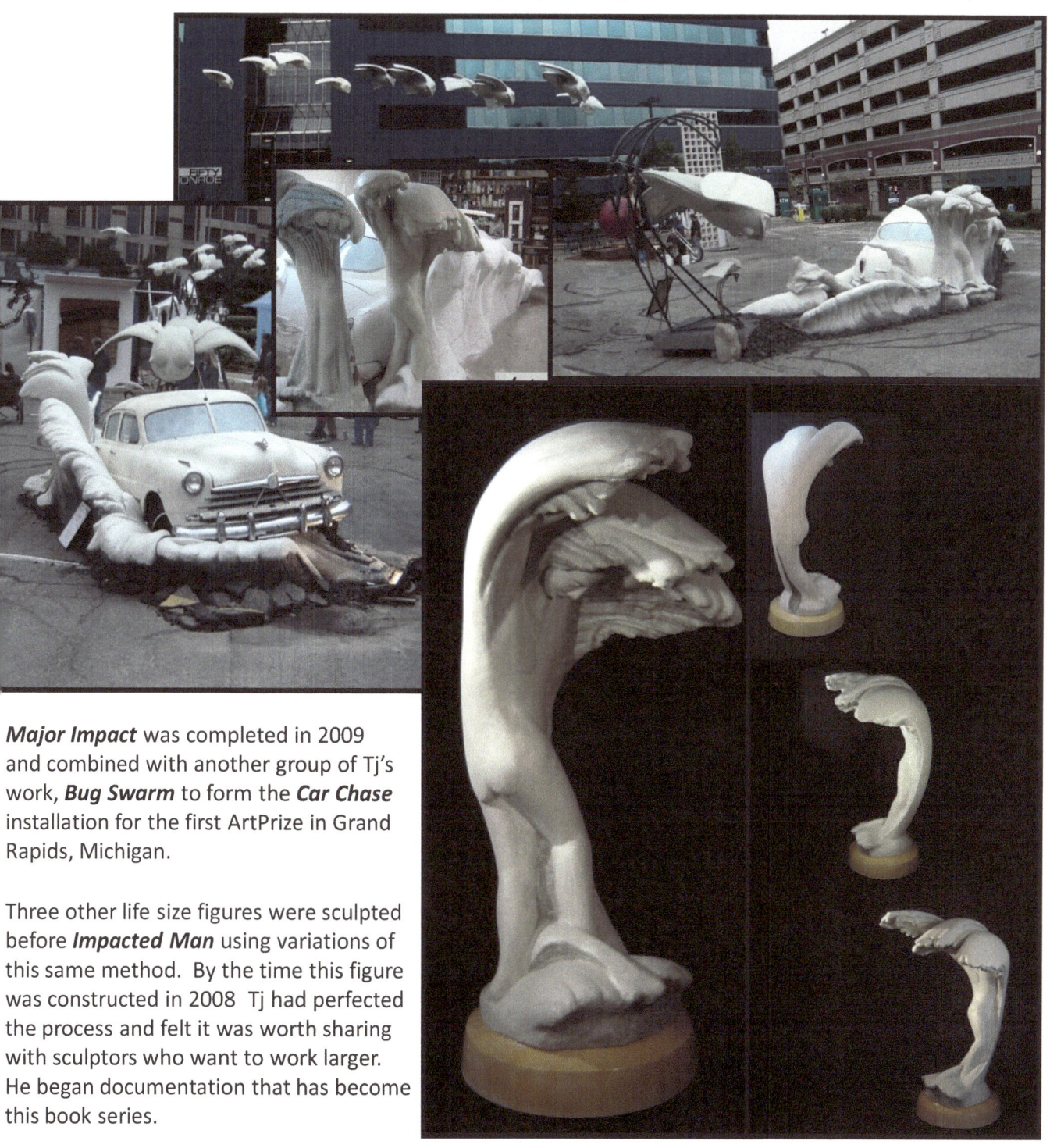

Major Impact was completed in 2009 and combined with another group of Tj's work, ***Bug Swarm*** to form the ***Car Chase*** installation for the first ArtPrize in Grand Rapids, Michigan.

Three other life size figures were sculpted before ***Impacted Man*** using variations of this same method. By the time this figure was constructed in 2008 Tj had perfected the process and felt it was worth sharing with sculptors who want to work larger. He began documentation that has become this book series.

The Appendage Story!

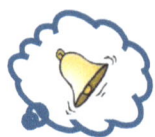

My craftsman's bell wasn't loud enough! This appendage joint was problematic throughout this build. At one point during coating I was carrying it through a doorway and whacked this appendage on the sill. I added glue to the crack but it had been weakened inside. Fast forward one year: *Impacted Man* is stone coated and finished. I was bringing it into the studio returning from a regional show. (Two of us carrying it). The long arm created by this protruding block cracked, and I took it off. It broke cleanly along the joint. I drilled two ¾ inch holes (positions indicated in red) right through the whole form and mudded in dowel pins with 5 minute epoxy. Both interior sides of the joining area were troweled with epoxy as well. The appendage was replaced and the surface finish was reworked. I V cut the surface and added extra strong glass filled cement to the patch joint and a bit of extra material to the surfaces around this joint. Fortunately these materials match up and the repair is not visible.

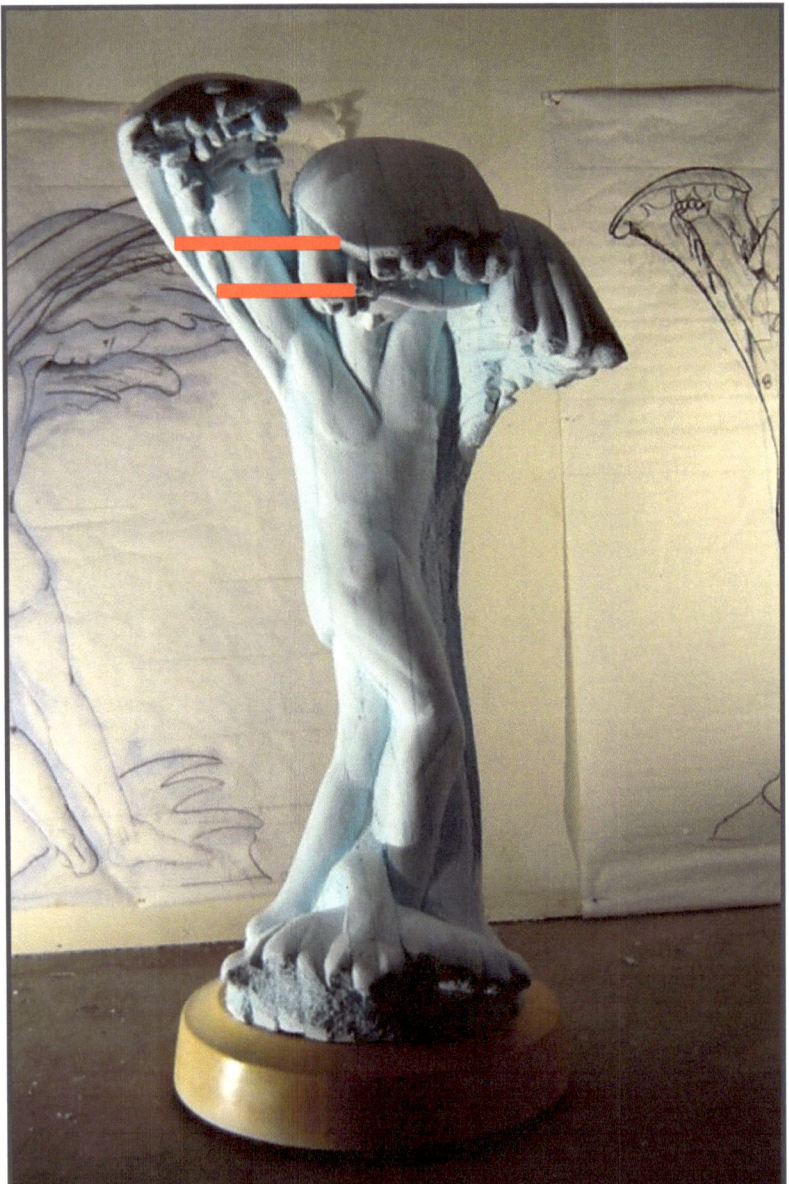

In perfect hind sight I now see the proper method would be to add those dowel pins and extra glue at the point when carving is finished and the exterior coating is about to be applied. At this point in the process we are done with carving and out of danger of running into hard glue. The patching of a couple of dowel holes with foam plugs is a simple task before finishes are applied, unlike the repair job that I had to do.

This incident also led to a stronger outer coating material that would also have prevented the break. More on that in Book 3.

Oh well, another one for the "Lessons Learned" file, but it's to your gain.

About the Author

Tj Aitken   Installation Artist

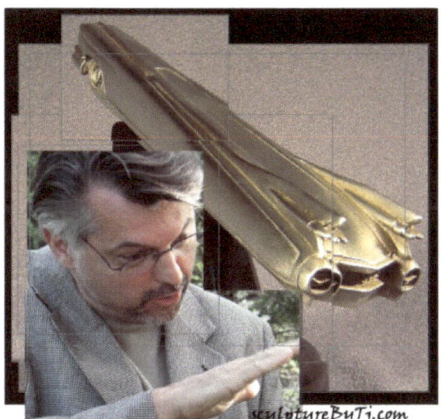

Tj does sculpture installations, workshops and consults on creativity management with his company Novus Resource. He writes on art themes and for "how to" books. The sculpture theme:
"The Impact of the Auto on Human Society" is his passion.

His installations include: Grand Rapids Public Museum ArtPrize 2010, and ArtPrize 2009 (top 25) - *Sculpture in the Square* Installation Troy Ohio, Solo Show Logsdon 1909 Chicago 2008, Marshal M. Fredricks Sculpture Museum biennial show award 08, *Velocity*- International Invitational Minneapolis MN 2008, *Eyes on Design* top art prize Grosse Pt. MI 07. He has spoken on quantifying aesthetics at the Harvard *Front end of Innovation* conference, the Innovation Network, and the Creative Problem Solving Institute's annual conferences

Tj was a design director for a fortune 300 automotive company. He worked in Europe in the 90's setting up design studios and managing projects. He has lectured world wide, training thousands of engineers in managing aesthetics. He holds design and process patents and his materials have been translated into 5 languages. He now applies his expertise as a design director and prototype build manager to the world of sculpture. He can be contacted through his website at: **www.sculpturebytj.com**